WINNING ISN'T LUCK

Fred Imhoff

Translated by Chris Schram

WINNING ISN'T LUCK

How to Succeed in Racing Dinghies and Yachts

ADLARD COLES NAUTICAL

BLOOMSBURY
LONDON · OXFORD · NEW YORK · NEW DELHI · SYDNEY

Adlard Coles Nautical
An imprint of Bloomsbury Publishing Plc

50 Bedford Square
London
WC1B 3DP
UK

1385 Broadway
New York
NY 10018
USA

www.bloomsbury.com

ADLARD COLES, ADLARD COLES NAUTICAL and the Buoy logo
are trademarks of Bloomsbury Publishing Plc

British Library Cataloguing-in-Publication Data
A catalogue record for this book is available from the British Library.
Library of Congress Cataloguing-in-Publication data has been applied for.

ISBN: PB: 978-1-4729-2246-5
ePDF: 978-1-4729-2609-8
ePub: 978-1-4729-2608-1

2 4 6 8 10 9 7 5 3 1

Typeset in 8.75 on 13.5pt TheSerif by Susan McIntyre
Printed and bound in China by RRD Asia Printing Solutions Limited

Bloomsbury Publishing Plc makes every effort to ensure that the papers used in the manufacture of
our books are natural, recyclable products made from wood grown in well-managed forests.
Our manufacturing processes conform to the environmental regulations of the country of origin.
To find out more about our authors and books visit www.bloomsbury.com. Here you will find extracts,
author interviews, details of forthcoming events and the option to sign up for our newsletters.

Note: while all reasonable care has been taken in the publication of this book, the publisher
takes no responsibility for the use of the methods or products described in the book.

Photographs by Thom Touw, Jan Faber, Eric van Staten, Ineke Schipstra and Ben Rutte

The following photographs are © Thom Touw: p2–3, p5, p8, p12, p14, p16, p17, p19,
p20, p22–3, p25, p26, p30, p34, p37, p38, p39, p40, p43, p44, p47, p48, p62, p67, p76,
p78, p79, p86, p88, p90, p91, p92, p98, p100, p102, p104, p105, p110, p120, p121, p125,
p126. www.thomtouw.com

Note: For ease of reading, unspecified people are referred to as 'he' or 'him' throughout this book.
However, the person concerned could equally be female or male.

contents

introduction

SAILBOAT RACING IS THE MOST COMPLEX SPORT AROUND – AND LIFE IS FAR TOO SHORT TO EVER FULLY MASTER IT. I WROTE THIS BOOK TO SAVE YOU TIME ON THE LONG ROAD TO BECOMING A SUCCESSFUL COMPETITION SAILOR, AND ESPECIALLY TO SPARE YOU FROM HAVING TO REINVENT THE WHEEL – SOMETHING THAT WOULD COST AN AWFUL LOT OF MONEY AND TAKE A LONG TIME.

Therefore you will not find tedious theories and exhausting descriptions of complicated details here, but instead clear descriptions of the most important elements of racing, and how to use them as quickly as possible to improve your results.

I will only focus on the knowledge you'll need to be able to make the right decisions in different situations and leave out anything irrelevant to racing. Thus, useless information transfer is avoided and more time can be spent on the things that can directly contribute to your racing success.

For example, the tides are caused by the gravitational force of the moon. Is this knowledge useful in racing? No! Therefore, just accept the tides as they are. When the tide turns, the wind changes in force and/or direction. Is that useful for sailors to know? Yes! It is important to know how this happens so that we can predict it and use it to our advantage.

Whether dealing with dinghies or keel boats, short upwind/downwind courses or offshore races, the topics addressed in this book apply to all types of sailing, although priorities may differ. So the most important thing is to learn a certain way of thinking; to

approach everything logically; and to prioritise and weigh different aspects objectively. Everything about competition sailing is logical, but it's still complicated because there are so many factors to take into account.

Good or bad luck has very little to do with any of this. It's a question of missed signs and misinterpreted signals – and these stem from a lack of knowledge. Most sailors have their own ways of prioritising, but they tend to fall back on their strengths. They may excel in strategy, sail trim, meteorology, the racing rules or the use of instruments because they enjoy or are good at that, but they tend to neglect other aspects because they find them difficult or don't like them as much. Try to keep everything in perspective and learn more about the topics you're less good at. To win you need to excel in everything, including the things you don't enjoy as much.

Because the sport is so complicated, you have to eliminate as many irrelevant details as possible and try not to get totally wrapped up in the nitty-gritty of speed and equipment. You don't need to be faster than the others; matching their speed is enough.

You just need to sail better, make fewer mistakes and take advantage of other people's mistakes – because everyone will make them.

I would like to thank my old marine engineering study mate and sailboat racer in heart and soul, Lex Keuning, without whose help I could never have explained the workings of sails as clearly. He also corrected errors and made improvements with his precise editing. Many thanks also to Henk Plaatje, for whom it was no trouble at all to add little details or make changes to the images to achieve optimal results, and Thom Touw, whose vast archive provided the most fantastic photos to choose from.

Fred Imhoff

chapter 1

establishing priorities

FUNDAMENTALLY, YOU CAN DRAW ALL ASPECTS OF SAILBOAT RACING AS A BIG UMBRELLA – START WITH THE MAIN SUBJECTS, AND THEN SUBDIVIDE THESE FURTHER. THE DIAGRAMS ON PAGES 10 AND 11 DEPICT THIS BIG UMBRELLA. AS AN EXAMPLE, LET US FURTHER EXPLORE THE TOPIC 'UPWIND SAIL TRIM'. THIS TOPIC ALONE CAN BE SUBDIVIDED INTO:

▶ Genoa luff tension
▶ Genoa fairlead position
▶ Barber hauler position
▶ Genoa sheet tension
▶ Forestay tension
▶ Mainsail foot tension
▶ Mainsail cunningham eye position
▶ Sail batten stiffness
▶ Backstay tension
▶ Running backstay tension
▶ Genoa and/or mainsail leech lines
▶ Position of the traveller car
▶ Boom vang tension
▶ Mast bend
▶ Angle of the spreaders
▶ Upper shroud tension
▶ Lower shroud tension
▶ Pre-bend at deck level

If we further subdivide each of these topics, we end up with an overwhelming number of trim combinations, so the chances of selecting the ideal combination under different circumstances become negligible. As I said before, life is too short, especially when you are not a professional and you are sailing in a class with many trimming options. Soon it will become a matter of luck if you ever reach a 'reasonable' combination of all these factors. Once you realise this, you'll benefit from teaching yourself a logical way of thinking and establishing priorities. In the following chapters key aspects of sailboat racing will be covered, where I will further explain and apply this process.

Another way to shorten the learning curve is to eliminate all the less important details. In other words, make the umbrella smaller. This will not only save you a lot of time, it will also prevent the loss of concentration that often causes a sailboat racer to miss important things. Even the most focused individuals can maintain their concentration for only limited periods, and regattas usually take longer than many other sporting matches. If you start focusing on all the trim possibilities you will quickly reach 'information overload', and it will become impossible to maintain your concentration during a whole race, let alone during a few shorter races over the course of a day.

Consequently, it is crucial to prioritise objectively in preparing for a race, as well as during a race. Ask yourself, what is more important: benefitting from stronger tide or a possible favourable change in wind direction? Trimming to point higher or going for speed? All too often, these decisions are made emotionally or based on whether or not something has worked previously. These, however, are really not the best ways to make your decisions.

The big umbrella of competition sailing.

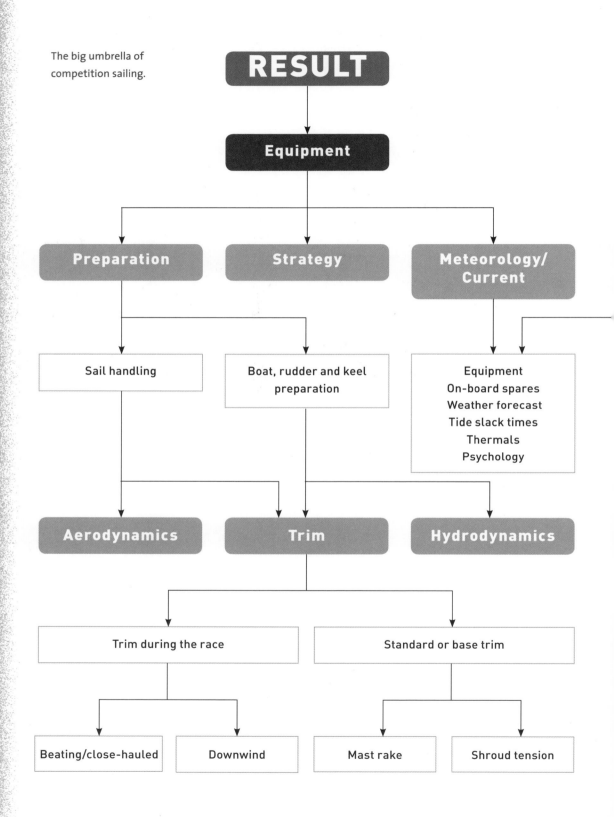

RESULT

Equipment

Preparation

Strategy

Meteorology/ Current

Sail handling

Boat, rudder and keel preparation

Equipment
On-board spares
Weather forecast
Tide slack times
Thermals
Psychology

Aerodynamics

Trim

Hydrodynamics

Trim during the race

Standard or base trim

Beating/close-hauled

Downwind

Mast rake

Shroud tension

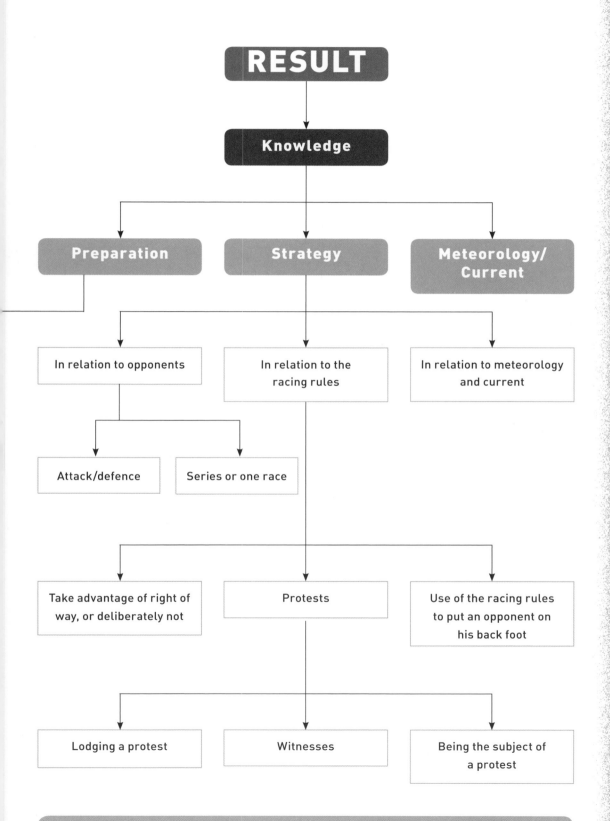

chapter 2

preparation

PREPARATION CAN BE DIVIDED INTO FOUR PARTS: TRAINING, EQUIPMENT PREPARATION, MENTAL PREPARATION AND PHYSICAL PREPARATION. ALL FOUR ASPECTS ARE IMPORTANT.

TRAINING

Use training to try to eliminate ingrained human reactions that can be a disadvantage in competition. For example, when a crew is concentrating on spinnaker trimming and the helmsman says something to him, he turns to look at the helmsman and responds. This is a typical human reaction – you normally look at someone when you respond to them. In a sail race this is completely wrong!

You have ears to listen with, a mouth to speak with, and eyes to look at what you are busy with. Otherwise the concentration of the crew on the spinnaker is disturbed, and at that moment the spinnaker can collapse, a gust can be missed, or you won't catch a wave on which you could have surfed nicely ahead. Therefore, in setting priorities it is better to spend a few hours training than spending time waxing the boat before each race so that it looks nice and shiny. Another well-accepted human trait is to do the things first that are easy and where you see an immediate result – in racing this is also wrong!

As a training exercise, you can call out that a boat behind has capsized or has been dismasted. A professional crew may ask questions or comment, but they will not look back at the other boat as they are focused on their tasks.

Go out training on a dark, moonless night. In doing so everyone learns how to find lines, cleats and jammers by touch, so that during a race they can work the lines without having to look away from the spinnaker or genoa.

Practise tacking quickly after rounding the leeward mark. We would lay a buoy around 20 metres from a sea wall, so that you had to tack within 20 metres of the rounding – otherwise your half-tonner or Dragon would sail into a concrete wall. In the beginning the tacking manoeuvres were not smartly executed, and the foredeck was not fully tidied up from the downwind leg. But after a few evening training sessions, and evaluating afterwards how to improve, we had it nailed – and the ability to tack quickly after the buoy frequently gave us an advantage in races.

Finally, train for situations where something has gone wrong. For example, you are just short of making the upwind buoy but the spinnaker pole is already set. Tacking is not an option due to other boats and the pole is in the way. Let the crew consider the options, and no doubt someone will come up with a solution – quickly furl the jib, so that you can point nearly directly in the wind without the jib backwinding and the boat starting to tack. The spinnaker pole can remain up, so that the spinnaker can be hoisted immediately after rounding. Practise this several times, so the crew will automatically react correctly when faced with the same situation during a race.

No concentration by the helmsman and crew. More attention on the distant camera than on the spinnaker. Lines trailing in the water.

EQUIPMENT PREPARATION

Prevent losing through equipment breakage. Carry sufficient spares when racing – a few shackles, a block, tape, hand tools, extra lines and, on keel boats (even smaller ones, like the Soling, H-Boat or Dragon), a bosun's chair. Make sure everyone knows where the spares are stored, and discuss who does what in different problem scenarios: who will go up the mast, who will hoist him up, what course the helm will hold with the man aloft and so forth. Then practise each scenario. I've seen enough times that this is the difference between winning and losing a championship.

Mark all lines, as well as the traveller track, genoa rail and other controls. It is much easier to say 'Set it on 3' or 'on red' than giving constant advice: 'Harden that up a little ... no, that is too much ... OK, maybe a little bit more.' Additionally, without marking the settings, you can never reproduce them directly after rounding the bottom mark, or at the start. Someone who has selected all of the correct settings just before the start will frequently gain a length or more in the first minute after the start, will sail in clean air, and you will never catch them again.

After each race, record the settings that you used, as well as the sails, and note the wind speed, wave height and temperature (for a given wind speed there is less force at higher temperatures than at lower temperatures). The easiest method is to enter this data in a spreadsheet via a laptop. You can always go back to this data and determine which sail to use in different conditions and which trim settings were faster or slower. Yes, I know this requires discipline – but it works!

After winning a race the first beer beckons, no less so than the first comforting beer after a loss. Enjoy them a little later, but get the crew together as soon as possible after the race to record the data. Do not confuse speed with the result. You may have had very good boat speed but made the wrong tactical decisions, or you may have had so-so speed but were the only boat to benefit from a shift on one tack, or take better advantage of the current. Most of all, document the races where your speed was poor – so that under the same circumstances in the future you do not use the same unhelpful combination of settings!

MENTAL PREPARATION

Solid mental preparation before a race is essential. Making a split-second tactical decision, seeing a situation develop well in advance, recognising early that the wind strength or direction is changing, knowing what an opponent will do if you tack or gybe … you can only do these things well if your mind is a blank slate before the race. You can't be thinking, even subconsciously, about your work, an argument with your spouse, family problems, or your mistress.

How can you manage this? Naturally it works differently for everyone, but what works for most people is arriving early at the race venue. Not for training or further boat preparation, as these are things you should already have done. If they still need to be done when you arrive, it is too late. Instead, try to read a book, relax outside a café with coffee, and play games. In short, act like you are on vacation and clear your mind.

You might also explore the area and discuss with your crew how thermals might develop, potential shore effects, and how the current behaves.

I knew a top international sailor who was by far the best in his class in Holland, but without fail he would lose the first race of the day on Saturday. It turned out that every Saturday morning he would go into the office for a few hours before leaving for the race. It was obvious that he didn't have his head in the race until the afternoon, and that is why he continued to lose on that day. Of course, you might argue that to stay away from the office on your free day costs money, that's understandable – but buying new sails and gear also costs money.

Above all, training costs time. You will never win unless you put in the effort – just look at what other athletes do to reach the top level internationally. Of course, everyone must have his own idea of how far he wants to go; I can provide advice on how to improve your results quickly, on the national as well as international level, but your goals and how you can achieve them is ultimately up to you.

Avoid stress, and train to minimise it. Stress in a sail race is your greatest opponent. I have seen heart surgeons, engineers and businessmen make the most childish mistakes because they were stressed out. An experienced sailor, with a range of championships to his name, held second place at the top mark in the final race. He only had to finish in the top 20 of 38 to secure the

Super concentration and perfect boat handling during a gybe.

championship. Just after hoisting the spinnaker, the halyard broke. The two crew hauled the spinnaker back in and looked defeated, and were further disheartened as they sailed back to the harbour. The championship was lost! In the moment of stress they did not think they could drop the jib and rehoist the spinnaker on the jib halyard, and just before the bottom mark they could change back.

PHYSICAL PREPARATION

This is very much dependent on your type of boat: dinghy, keel boat or offshore racing yacht. On a dinghy it is important that you can hike out for extended periods without muscle pain or cramps. If not, you will lose concentration, so work on your stomach and thigh muscles.

On keel boats there are higher loads on the control lines, and you need to train your shoulder and arm muscles accordingly. Find a good trainer or physiotherapist, explain precisely your function on board, and let him devise a training programme for you. That will prevent a host of injuries, as well as bad knees and back problems later in life.

For longer races on an offshore racing yacht, stamina is key; ensure you are well rested and in good condition before you begin.

Make sure you have appropriate food and drink available throughout the race. Failure to drink enough during a race, or between races if there are more than one in a day, will lead to a huge loss of concentration.

FINALLY

Immerse yourself again in working with vectors. This is required for selection of lines and deck gear, because you need to know the loads on blocks, fittings and lines. You can avoid selecting gear that is too heavy, and instead choose the lightest possible equipment that is still sufficiently strong.

Vectors are also important in meteorology, to combine wind components, as well as for sailing in current. Without a basic under-standing of vectors there is a host of things in sailing you will not understand, let alone being able to predict wind shifts and the effects of current. For example, how can you determine if you will be in the foul air or wind shadow of a competitor, or if you can blanket an opponent, without understanding vectors? You can't – and instead you wait for it to happen.

A brief refresher for those of you who have not worked with vectors in a long time. You can represent a force, such as the speed and direction of the wind or current, with an arrow. The direction of the arrow is the direction of the force (current or wind), and the length of the arrow is proportional to the force (see Fig 1).

Good physical fitness improves concentration and the will to win.

The wind is shown as arrow A. The speed of the boat creates an opposing wind, arrow B. If we want to determine the 'apparent wind' – which is what the windvane atop the mast shows us – we need to add arrows A and B. Arrows A and B both originate from the same point. Draw a dotted line from the arrowhead of arrow A, parallel to and the same length as arrow B. Next draw a dotted line from the head of arrow B, parallel to and the same length as arrow A. Now draw an arrow from the beginning point of arrows A and B to the intersection of the two dotted lines. This arrow 'C' is the addition of arrows A and B – in other words, the apparent wind. Further, this arrow shows the direction and force of the apparent wind.

You can also subtract vectors (see Fig 2). The current is shown by vector S, and we would like to determine how much it helps push us forward and how much it will force us leeward. Draw one dotted line from the head of arrow S, parallel to the centreline of the boat, and a second dotted line from the head, perpendicular to the centreline. From the start point of arrow S, draw one arrow parallel and one arrow perpendicular to the centreline of the boat, to intersect the dotted lines. This has split the current vector into two components, the current in the direction of travel of the boat (A) and the perpendicular component of current pushing the boat leeward (B).

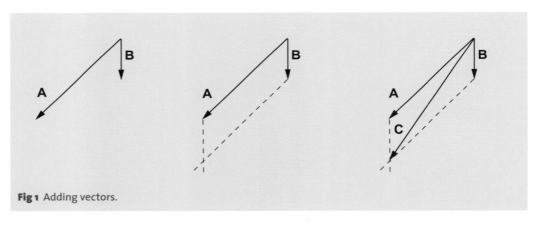

Fig 1 Adding vectors.

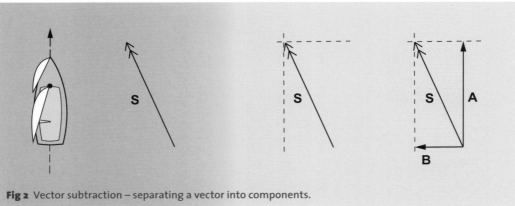

Fig 2 Vector subtraction – separating a vector into components.

IN SUMMARY:

- ▶ Eliminate all irrelevant details
- ▶ Teach yourself to concentrate
- ▶ Continually weigh priorities
- ▶ Train to overcome human reactions that have a negative impact on racing
- ▶ Prevent losing through mistakes and so-called 'bad luck'
- ▶ Avoid stress
- ▶ Mark all adjustable fittings and lines
- ▶ Document settings and other relevant information after each race
- ▶ (Re)familiarise yourself with vector calculations

chapter 3

equipment

YOU CAN COMPARE A SAILBOAT WITH A CAR: THE HULL IS THE CHASSIS, THE SAILS ARE THE ENGINE, THE MAST, BOOM AND SHROUDS ARE THE ENGINE MOUNTS AND WIND IS THE FUEL.

How do you buy a car? Normally you would consider a range of factors, such as size, maintenance costs, trade-in value, safety and comfort. Why wouldn't you do the same when buying a boat?

Should you purchase new or second-hand? A larger, used luxury car is frequently less costly than a smaller new car, but is usually more expensive to run and maintain. You can use similar criteria in determining the type (and class) of boat to purchase.

For competition, do you want to go off-road, compete in rallies, or race on a track? This helps define the choices available, and the same applies to racing boats. Do you want to race offshore, in a one-design fleet, an international class, or stay in your home waters and take part in club racing?

I'll assume that you want to reach the top in your class and not remain with the back markers, or over the years become a steady mid-pack finisher. Why else would you be reading this book?

This begs the first question: do I need to buy a new boat? No, of course not! New isn't always better. The salesman at the car dealer will always tell you that he has the latest model available. If you ask him what is so much improved over the old model, his eyes will first go blank, and then he'll reiterate that this is the very latest model, equipped with the newest technology, and that is why it is more costly. After more extensive questioning he may recall that the grill has been restyled, and the rear lights are a slightly different shape. There must be some visual differences, right?

The same happens with race boats, because boatbuilders prefer to sell new boats. On the other hand, it isn't worth purchasing something that at the end of the day will not be fast enough – that would be penny wise and pound foolish. If you lose a few metres in the minutes after the start due to less speed, you'll find yourself in foul air and continuously forced to tack and sail on the less favoured side. You'll find yourself habitually falling behind, learning nothing and enjoying it less and less. So buy a boat that is equivalent to what the top international sailors in your class have. The same applies to your mast and sails. If you have the same equipment you can manage the same speed, and win by making fewer mistakes. Above all, you won't have to worry about the choice, relieving any insecurity and providing peace of mind.

As for sails, it is even clearer that the latest model isn't necessarily the best. Not long ago (December 2012) I spoke with a sailmaker friend, who represents one of the largest international lofts. He told me that they had recently resurrected some old designs from 1994 and 1995, because all of their newer

It is likely that boats 715 and 645 are sailing with the same type of jib, except it looks like the one on 645 is ready for a replacement; with a loose leech 645 will never sail as high as 715.

designs proved to be slower than the old design and they were losing clients. Now they make some unnecessary changes every year to some seams, as well as the shape of the window. Just like the latest car model!

Ultimately, sails are different from a boat. They are subject to harder wear, just like the tyres on a racing car. Top international sailors often use a new set for each important competition and order three to five sets at a time. I'm not sure if this is entirely necessary, but if you want to race seriously and have the resources, a new mainsail, two genoas or jibs and a spinnaker would be advisable each season.

The sailmaker will also try to sell you different sails for different weather conditions and circumstances: one set for light weather, another for medium conditions, and yet another for heavy weather. And perhaps even the same story for sailing in waves or on flat water. My experience is that you are better off with a solid all-around set, and with a new spare set on hand. Let me further explain why.

I do not recommend extreme light wind sails for the following reasons:

1. If there is truly very light wind, seeking out patches of wind and taking advantage of shifts is more important than a fraction more speed.

2. In light wind there is a good chance that more wind will come (and you will have the wrong sails up), or that the race will be cancelled.

3. Light wind sails usually have the same form and size but are made out of lighter material, and hence are advantageous only on flat water. If there is swell or waves the lightweight cloth will move and flap more easily, while heavier sailcloth will better hold its form (profile).

I also do not believe in specific heavy weather sails, more or less for similar reasons. As soon as the wind drops, you are caught out with slower sails, and if the wind increases the race is cancelled. Also, the flatter cut sails are a problem in steep waves as they do not have as much drive to power through them. Finally, you can trim an all-around sail for heavy wind conditions, assuming the cloth is heavy enough (low stretch).

I've frequently come across individuals who have their boat specially built, purchase different sails from what is generally available, experiment with masts and so forth. I can't say that I've actually seen many great leaps forward as a result of this. Frequently a lack of self-confidence leads to trying different sails, or a hobby gets out of hand so that only one element of sailboat racing is explored, and this becomes a very expensive gamble. Developing new and faster equipment is generally the domain of the top boats in an international class, where all elements of racing are already well in hand and there is time to delve deeply into these new developments.

In summary, purchase up-to-date equipment, but gear that is well proven. And as I noted earlier, keep it as simple as possible, because sailboat racing is already difficult enough. I hope for many of you that I have not dashed your ambitions to become a champion, because one thing is certain: you do not win only by buying the latest or best equipment!

As regards to your budget, here are some rules of thumb:

1. If you have a hypothetical budget of 100, then purchase a boat (new or second-hand) for 50. You then have enough budget to bring the boat into top condition, and can purchase extra sails, boat covers, fittings, gear, instruments and so on to ensure that everything works optimally.

2. Be prepared to spend 25 (half the initial boat investment) on annual costs, including depreciation, new sails, replacing lines and deck gear, entry fees, mooring costs, insurance and travel costs. If it is a small boat and you are competing internationally, count on a slightly higher percentage for your running costs. This is based on no paid crew, and therefore they will be individually responsible for their own travel and accommodation costs.

Of course, these are general rules, but establishing a budget for sailboat racing in a given class each season, and maintaining a reasonable amount for contingencies, will avoid the huge disappointment associated with lack of funding derailing your campaign to become a champion.

Consider also from the beginning the layout and fittings. Equip and configure the boat (within the class rules) as functionally and ergonomically as possible. Ensure you can operate all lines and running without unnecessary movement around the boat, and without impairing the sight lines of the helmsman or spinnaker trimmer. Failing either can be annoying and uses unnecessary energy.

For example, you can mount the barber haulers such that during a gybe a crew can, in one fluid movement through 180 degrees, first pull in on the lee barber hauler, take hold of the mainsheet and guide the boom over, and finally let out on the windward barber hauler.

If a crew needs to go forward to set, gybe or take down the spinnaker pole and the cockpit is deep, install a step for them.

On smaller boats, mount the spinnaker blocks such that during the hoist, gybe or drop a crew can also hand the spinnaker

Trimming the boat to reduce wetted surface in light conditions.

sheets to the helmsman. At this moment the helmsman has the best view forward, and he can even hold the tiller between his knees.

Ensure that when they are hiking, or sitting on the low side in light conditions, it is as comfortable as possible for the crew. Take into account that each crewmember needs to have clear sight for their specific tasks, whether helming or trimming the spinnaker or genoa.

Always bear in mind the fore-aft weight distribution of the crew. In light weather the crew can be shifted forward to reduce the surface area of the hull underwater, while at higher speed the crew can be moved further aft to lengthen the waterline. Also try to position the helmsman and crew as closely together as possible, because concentrating crew weight in the centre of the boat and having less weight at the ends results in a more efficient movement in waves. Finally, document the optimal fore- and aft locations of the crew at different speeds.

CLARKE
BJORN

chapter 4

the forces on fittings and lines

IT IS USEFUL FOR THE SAILBOAT RACER TO UNDERSTAND THE FORCES ON DIFFERENT DECK GEAR, LINES AND BLOCKS. HOW STRONG DOES EACH TYPE OF BLOCK OR ITEM OF DECK GEAR NEED TO BE? IN OTHER WORDS, WHAT ARE THE WORKING LOADS? A NOTED SAILING HARDWARE MANUFACTURER OFFERS A SIMPLE ONLINE PROGRAM TO MAKE THESE CALCULATIONS, BUT IT IS ALSO HELPFUL TO KNOW HOW THESE ARE CALCULATED, AS THIS IS AN AREA OF FREQUENT MISUNDERSTANDING.

A common mistake is to assume that the highest loads on the genoa sheet, genoa lead (car) and turning block occur when using the largest genoa. This is not correct, because while the force increases linearly based on surface area of the sail, the force is also proportional to the square of the wind speed.

There is one more factor that influences the load: the angle between the genoa sheet and the lead. For a 150% genoa, this angle is usually around 30–45 degrees, while it is closer to 60 degrees for a no.3, no.4 or high-aspect jib. Fig 3 shows how this influences the force on the genoa lead.

In Fig 4, you can see the forces on the various turning blocks and the winch. With a maximum force of 700kg on the genoa sheet, we have the following options:

▶ A genoa lead for no.3 and 4 with a work-load of 1 x 700kg (+50% safety margin for friction and shock) = 1,050kg

▶ A genoa lead for the no.1 with a workload of (1:2.6) x 0.73 x 700kg (+50% safety margin) = 295kg

▶ A turning block 1 for the no.3 and 4 with a workload of 2 x 1 x 700kg (+50%) = 2,100kg

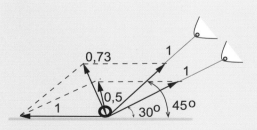 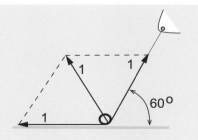

Fig 3 The forces on a genoa lead. For the no.1, the angle between sheet and deck is about 30–45 degrees; the force on the lead is 0.50–0.73 times the force on the sheet. For the no.3 and 4, the angle between sheet and deck is 60 degrees; the force on the lead is the same as the force on the sheet.

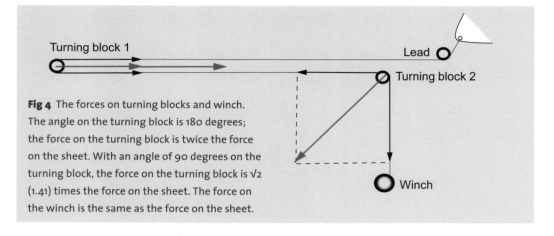

Fig 4 The forces on turning blocks and winch. The angle on the turning block is 180 degrees; the force on the turning block is twice the force on the sheet. With an angle of 90 degrees on the turning block, the force on the turning block is √2 (1.41) times the force on the sheet. The force on the winch is the same as the force on the sheet.

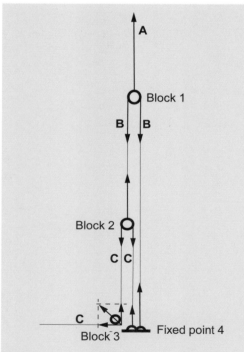

Fig 5 The forces on a compound tackle. Compound tackles, such as an adjustable backstay, come in all sorts of shapes and sizes depending on the boat and on the forces on the blocks and lines (the force on block 1 = A; the force on block 2 and anchor point (pad eye) 4 is B = 0.5 × A; the force on block 3 is C = 0.25 × A × √2, or (C=0.5 × B).

▶ A turning block 1 for the no.1 with a workload of 2 × (1:2.6) × 700kg (+50%) = 808kg

▶ A turning block 2 for the no.3 and 4 with a workload of 700kg × √2 (+50%) = 1,470kg

▶ A turning block 2 for the no.1 with a workload of 700kg × (1:2.6) × √2 (+50%) = 565kg

For the winch, we use a standard winch handle with a load of 20kg and a 20% loss of friction:

$$\frac{700\text{kg (maximum workload)}}{0.8 \text{ (friction of 20\%)} \times 20\text{kg}} = 43.75$$
(load on the handle)

Hence, a 44-winch would be suitable in this situation.

Why am I bothering you with all these numbers and load calculations? Because using these simple formulas (along with some vector calculations) you can quantify the loads that come to bear, and with this knowledge you can save weight and cost without compromising safety.

Please note that all the values used above are approximate and randomly chosen. I'm only concerned with the methodology, which can significantly help the racer to make informed decisions about deck gear.

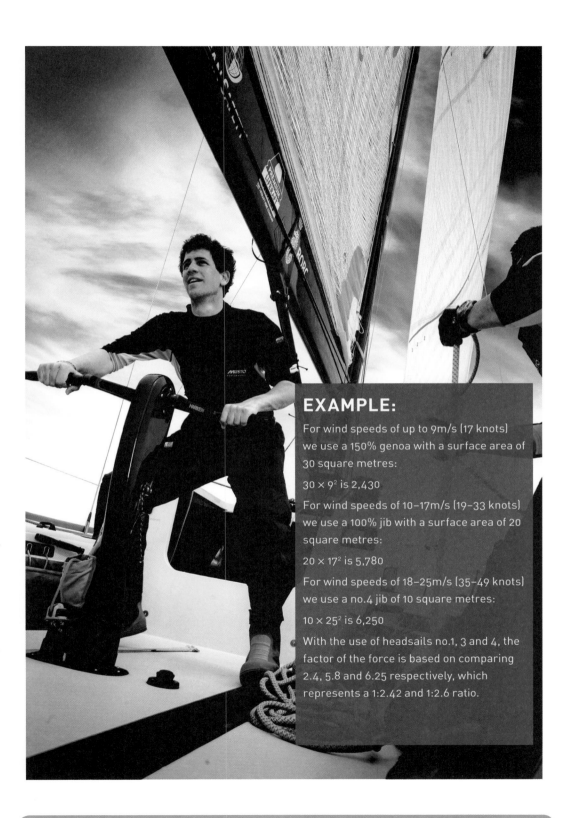

EXAMPLE:

For wind speeds of up to 9m/s (17 knots) we use a 150% genoa with a surface area of 30 square metres:

30×9^2 is 2,430

For wind speeds of 10–17m/s (19–33 knots) we use a 100% jib with a surface area of 20 square metres:

20×17^2 is 5,780

For wind speeds of 18–25m/s (35–49 knots) we use a no.4 jib of 10 square metres:

10×25^2 is 6,250

With the use of headsails no.1, 3 and 4, the factor of the force is based on comparing 2.4, 5.8 and 6.25 respectively, which represents a 1:2.42 and 1:2.6 ratio.

the how and why of trimming

TRIMMING A BOAT IS JUST LIKE GIVING MEDICINE: THERE IS AN ILLNESS AND YOU WANT TO CURE IT, OR IN ANY CASE YOU WANT TO REDUCE THE SYMPTOMS. THERE ARE DIFFERENT MEDICINES AVAILABLE TO TREAT AN ILLNESS, EACH WITH DIFFERENT SIDE EFFECTS, AND SO IT IS WITH TRIMMING. YOU WANT TO USE THE MEDICINE WITH THE FEWEST SIDE EFFECTS, OR WHERE THE SIDE EFFECTS CAN BE EASILY HANDLED.

If you want more forestay tension, you can tighten the running backstay. The side effects on a ⅞ fractional rig: less mainsheet tension, more tension on the jib or genoa luff, more mast bend, and reduced drive in chop. On a masthead rig you will have less mast bend, more tension on the jib or genoa luff, and less drive [acceleration] in chop.

You can also achieve it by pulling in the mainsheet, but with other side effects: more weather helm, the mainsail leech becomes tighter (and too closed), more luff tension on the jib or genoa, and less speed.

You can tighten the boom vang (kicker). This closes the mainsail leech, the mainsheet is slackened, and on smaller boats the lower part of the mast will bow forward due to the force of the boom against the mast. The luff of the jib or genoa will tighten.

Hardening the backstay has yet other side effects: less mainsheet tension, more mast bend, a flatter mainsail but more open at the top, and more tension on the jib or genoa luff.

On boats with shrouds angled aft to the deck and no backstay, such as the 505, Flying Dutchman or 470, you can tighten the shrouds. The side effects: less tension on the mainsheet and boom vang, but more tension on the luff of the jib or genoa. You can possibly cause more pre-bend in the mast if the spreaders are angled aft on the mast.

So here are five different medicines; each works as well as the other but with different side effects.

Another example: a close sailing friend rigged his boat (a Dragon) on the trailer with a new racing mast. Once he tightened the shrouds, the top of the mast was bent forward (see Fig 6A). Distraught, he looked around until he found a boatbuilder (and top sailor) from the same class. He explained his problem and asked for advice. His co-competitor thought about it and said, 'Move the point forward where the shrouds are attached to the deck, I've done that before when I experienced this problem.' He followed the advice and moved the shroud attachments so that they were slightly forward of the mast, and the mast top no longer bent forward (Fig 6B). My question to him was 'Do you really want your shroud attachments in that location?' My friend thought for a moment and said, 'No, not really.'

A multiple champion and company-sponsored sailor from the same class came by and my friend again described his problem. He answered, 'I would shift the mast foot a little bit aft on the mast track (Fig 6C), I've done that before and it worked.' My friend indeed tried it, and when the shrouds were tensioned the mast no longer bent forward. I again asked a question: 'Do you want the mast foot there? You've now increased the distance from the mast to the attachment point on the deck for the foresail, and to comply with the class rules (ie the 'J' measurement), you will have to move the attachment point for the foresail further aft. Do you really want that?'

The funny thing was that two top sailors in this international class had encountered the same problem and solved it in two different ways, but neither of them understood the underlying problem! The underlying problem was that the spreaders were angled too far forward. By moving the spreader tips slightly aft the problem was simply solved, without having to move either the shroud attachments forward or the mast foot aft (Fig 6D).

A further example, by way of comparison to another international sport: the world-champion Formula 1 driver pulls into the pits and tells his technical team: 'I need better acceleration, a higher top speed, less chassis lean in the turns and reduced understeer. Tighten a few screws and bolts and get this fixed.'

What do you think would happen next? Most likely the best driver in the world would be immediately and justifiably sacked. He instead needs to have a strong understanding of the engine and suspension, and the ability to clearly and precisely explain to the technical crew *what* needs to be adjusted, and *why*.

Hence it seems odd that racing sailors don't need to have a similar understanding. To put it more strongly, in many cases they do not even have a clue why a boat can sail upwind, instead of falling to lee or getting pushed backward. Taking it a step further – can your sailmaker, who is the designer and builder of your 'engine', explain this?

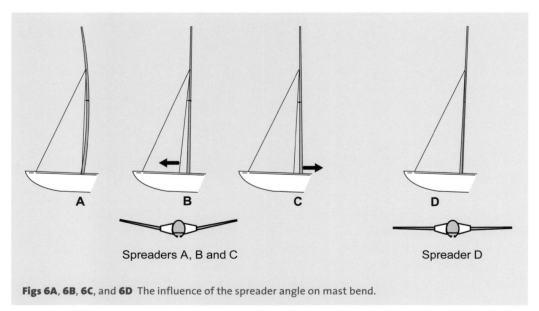

Figs 6A, **6B**, **6C**, and **6D** The influence of the spreader angle on mast bend.

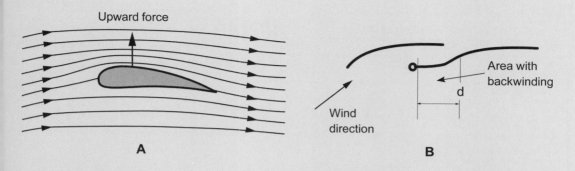

Fig 7A The working of an aeroplane wing.

Fig 7B The slot effect.

It's a strange situation, wouldn't you agree? Unfortunately, there are very few people who can provide a sensible answer to the question of why a boat can sail upwind. It is really too crazy for words – you need to tune your engine (trim your sails), but you don't understand how the engine works. Of course, everyone has some vague theories that come to mind, such as:

1. The classic comparison of a sail to an aeroplane wing, which provides lift (Fig 7A). Except people forget that the wing is not the same thickness over its cross section (unlike a sail), and this is what generates lift. The air takes a longer path along the curvature of the upper surface than the air passing below the wing, which creates a difference in air pressure above and below the wing, causing vertical lift. Additionally, the aeroplane engine drives the plane forward, and the wings only serve to provide the lift to counteract gravity.

If we apply this model to a sailboat, the lift would only push us leeward as there is no engine to drive us forward. Of course, you could respond 'But what about a glider?', but this also doesn't apply. It too has wings where the air has a longer path over the upper

surface than over the lower surface, but by falling toward the Earth, it generates forward motion. Even when it is lifted on a thermal it is dropping relative to the air around it.

2. The slot effect between the foresail and the main – also a nice story. The slot is a narrowing of the gap between the two sails, so that the air passes faster over the lee side of the mainsail and reduces the air pressure to lee.

Then why in heavier wind do we see the inside of the main getting backwinded by the foresail (Fig 7B)? It is because of higher pressure in the slot between the foresail and the main! Further, how can the Laser, Finn or Optimist sail upwind without a foresail? Think these things through before you begin trimming (or even ordering) your sails.

3. Finally, we have the story of the keel or centreboard, and how it generates lift to windward. But why? The form is the same on both sides (provided we are not setting the trim tab). Or do we instead perhaps see lift because the boat is moving to lee?

I'll come back to how it really works in Chapter 14.

weather helm

AS I ALREADY SAID IN THE INTRODUCTION, SAILBOAT RACING IS ENORMOUSLY
COMPLICATED. TOO COMPLICATED TO THINK YOU CAN EVER EXPLAIN IT IN A BOOK,
EVEN IF YOU LIMITED IT TO JUST TRIMMING. SO THE FOCUS IS ON SIMPLIFICATION –
IT'S ALL ABOUT YOUR WAY OF THINKING. I WILL SHARE A FEW EXAMPLES TO TRY TO
GIVE YOU FURTHER INSIGHT.

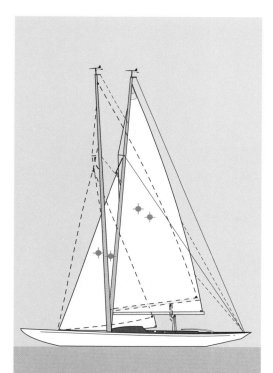

Fig 8 The effect of mast angle with respect
to the sail plan centre of effort. This extreme
change in mast angle only moves the centre of
effort 4% of the boat's length forward – but
your boat speed upwind will drop dramatically!

Sailors across many sailboat classes try to
reduce weather helm in heavier wind by
angling the mast further forward. In reality,
you are only moving the centre of force for the
sail area forward a minimal amount (see Fig 8,
for illustrative purposes showing an extreme
mast angle).

It is also a fact that as the wind increases a
sailboat is faster upwind with the mast raked
aft – whether we are talking about a DN
iceboat, Flying Dutchman, Dragon, or any
other class.

So in effect we are doing something that
reduces upwind speed, solely to solve another
problem: the weather helm. You are
prescribing the wrong medicine, but why?
Mainly by failing to understand the cause of
the disorder.

The underlying cause of weather helm isn't
heavy wind, but the heeling of the boat. The
sails serve as the boat's engine, and as long as
they remain above the centreline of the boat
there is no lee- or weather helm. If the boat
begins to heel you will shift the 'engine'
toward one side of the boat, and the boat will
more or less try to turn in a circle (see Fig 9).

Take a rowing boat and hang an outboard
motor on the stern, precisely on the
centreline, and the rowing boat will drive

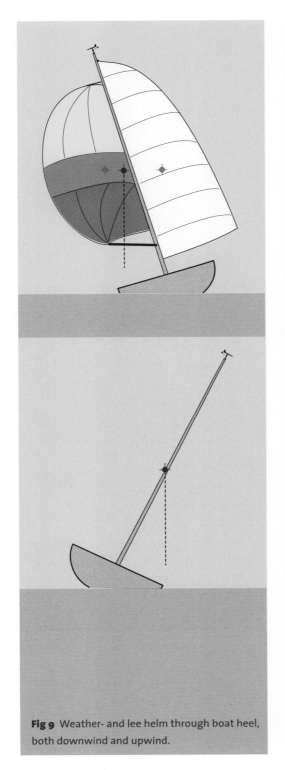

Fig 9 Weather- and lee helm through boat heel, both downwind and upwind.

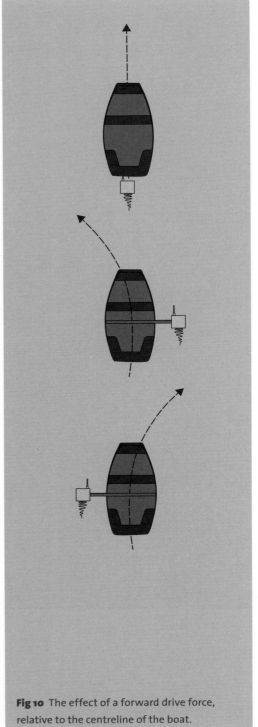

Fig 10 The effect of a forward drive force, relative to the centreline of the boat.

The centreboard raised a little and the boat sailing upright – perfect trim!

straight ahead. Now mount a beam across the centreline, and hang the motor outboard but parallel to the centreline. If you mount the motor on the right side, the boat will circle toward the left. If you mount it on the left, the boat will circle toward the right (Fig 10).

This is easy to try on a dinghy, where you can use your weight to steer the boat. Try this out: if you sit on the windward side to heel the boat to windward, it will bear away from the wind; if you move across and heel the boat to leeward, the boat will come up to the

wind; if you get the balance just right, the boat will move straight ahead. Rudder pressure to counter either lee- or weather helm serves as a huge brake.

Look again at what really happens if you angle the mast further forward. How far forward do you need to move the sail plan centre of effort? This does almost nothing compared to the effect of heel (Fig 8)! The medicine you must prescribe to reduce weather helm is now clear – trim and steer so that you have less heel.

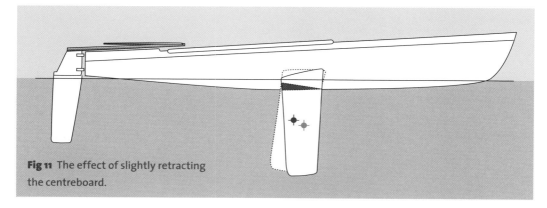

Fig 11 The effect of slightly retracting the centreboard.

The rudder is all the way over, but useless when the driving force of the sails is too far away from the centreline.

For the best upwind speed, the established rule is to angle the mast further forward in light conditions, and more mast rake in heavier wind. For dinghies with a centreboard that pivots on a pin, there is a second option – pull the centreboard up slightly when sailing upwind in a strong breeze. The centre of lateral resistance of the underwater portion of the centreboard moves slightly aft, without meaningfully reducing the area of the centreboard (Fig 11).

To summarise, you can manage weather helm as follows:

▶ Set the mast more upright, or angled slightly forward (disadvantages: less speed when sailing upwind in stronger wind and more leeway due to heel).

▶ When sailing upwind in a breeze on a boat with a pivoting centreboard, retract the centreboard slightly.

▶ Keep the boat more upright through trim and helming (advantages: higher speed and less leeway).

Of these the last two options are by far the most preferable.

In classes where adjusting the mast rake during a race is forbidden, we are grounded by reality, and I come back to the advice I gave earlier in the book: establish a good all-around setting and leave the mast rake alone. A further consideration: when running downwind, a mast that is raked forward is faster than one that is raked back or straight up. This is relatively simple in practice, by setting the mast adjuster on the deck forward, and slackening the backstay and/or runners when sailing downwind.

So why is this? I can continue with a detailed theoretical explanation, but this has little value as you will have to read through many pages about something for which we have no further use. So I will conveniently leave it in the category of established 'facts'.

Broaching when sailing downwind is governed by the same principles. If the boat is heeled to windward the engine, or the centre of effort of the sail plan, is also shifted to windward (Fig 9). The boat falls off the wind and makes a 'Chinese gybe', broaching to leeward. Bear in mind that most boats running in heavy wind broach to lee and end up gybing and knocked flat.

Naturally, there are things that can be done. Initially you can move crew to the leeward side. Then you can apply the trim 'medicine', to shift the 'engine' back toward the centreline of the boat. This can be accomplished by easing the boom vang, so that there is less pressure in the top of the mainsail (which may end up on the weather side of the boat anyway). You can also trim the sheet and guy closer, to prevent the spinnaker from rotating further to windward. The whole process of broaching to leeward and making a Chinese gybe (and ending up flat) is amplified by the centrifugal force generated when rounding to lee to the other tack.

Broaching to windward is more or less the same, also generating a centrifugal force that amplifies the heeling, except that the pressure goes out of the mainsail and spinnaker as soon as you round up.

If I could choose I'd rather broach to weather than broach to lee (along with the Chinese gybe). If you agree, then follow this advice. I know, it feels strange sitting on the lee side, but...

The helmsman sitting on the leeward side and the spinnaker sheeted tightly in. Perfect downwind trim in these heavy conditions.

chapter 7

trimming on waves

FOR MANY YEARS MY CREW AND I WERE THE FASTEST IN THE WORLD – WHETHER ON CENTREBOARD BOATS (FLYING DUTCHMAN) OR KEEL BOATS (DRAGON, QUARTER TONNER ETC) – IN HEAVY WEATHER AND SHORT WAVES ('CHOP'). I WAS NO BETTER A HELMSMAN THAN MANY OF THE PROFESSIONALS IN MY CLASS, NOR WAS MY EQUIPMENT BETTER. I THINK IT WAS MAINLY DUE TO OUR TRIM. LET ME EXPLAIN WHAT MY IDEAS WERE THEN … AND STILL ARE.

In chop, a sailboat moves up and down within a few seconds, and frequently the landing on the next wave is relatively hard ('slamming') – I'll come back to this later. What are the effects? First, the mast top swings forward when the boat hits the next wave and decelerates; it then recovers its form before swinging backward as the boat rides down the wave. All of this occurs within a few seconds. With a wind speed of 19 knots, the apparent wind speed in the top of the sail rises to 34 knots, and a few seconds later drops to 4 knots.

This effect is amplified by the top of the mast 'whipping' (Fig 12). Ultimately, it is too short a period to correct for the changing wind speeds at the top half of the sail. The mast whipping forward also completely closes the mainsail leech (which promotes heeling as well as reducing drive), and when the mast swings backward the leech becomes excessively open.

In short, the bow is pointing close to the wind, but with each wave a drop in speed and increased heel pushes the boat leeward. How can we correct this? Take a bamboo stick and

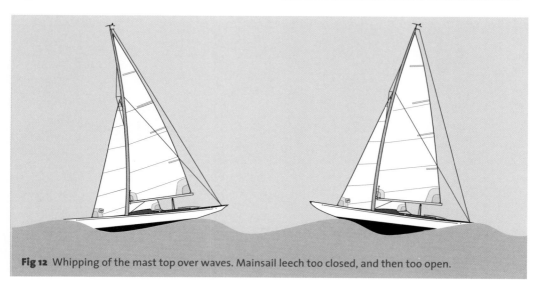

Fig 12 Whipping of the mast top over waves. Mainsail leech too closed, and then too open.

swing it quickly back and forth, and the tip will impressively whip further at each end of the motion. Now tie a string to each end of the stick, like on a bow for a bow-and-arrow. Now if you swing the stick back and forth, the end of the stick will not whip further. Let's apply this idea to our mast.

The same applies to the genoa: it should have enough twist in the top so that you can apply reasonable tension to the leech, with the fairlead moved as needed further out. Are the actions above a disadvantage in flat water and less wind? No, not at all. You can always move the traveller up to windward and ease the mainsheet. Further, you can set the mast adjuster further aft (or reset deck chocks) to align the mast straighter.

To keep it simple we will maintain one position with regards to mast rake, one type/set of sails, and a fixed setting for the shrouds. This gave us much peace of mind, so that we could concentrate on tactics vis-à-vis our competitors, wind shifts and current.

Simply put, we adjusted mast bend and the traveller in chop, as if we were sailing in flat water with a wind force 1–2 points greater.

Finally, keep in mind that:

▶ You can more easily close the leech in a sail that is open than the other way around.

▶ In my opinion the shroud tension is not important in light conditions, as in this case the only function for the shrouds is to keep the mast upright.

1. The mast base is fixed to the mast plate/track below deck.

2. On deck level we can establish pre-bend through a mast controller, or by chocks between the aft side of the mast and the deck opening.

3. Moving higher, the mast can be fixed at the height of the spreaders by angling the spreaders back (eg 4 or 5cm on a 7.5 metres shroud length).

4. The mast is further held rigid by upper shrouds and forestay.

5. Finally, we need to secure the top of the mast. For boats up to 9 or 10 metres, this can be accomplished through relatively high mainsheet tension (Fig 13). In this case, there are two things necessary for the mainsail to generate good drive: (a) the traveller is moved toward the leeward outer end, and (b) there should be enough twist in the top of the sail, so that the leech isn't excessively closed. You'll also need a mainsail with enough, but not excessive, rounding in the luff.

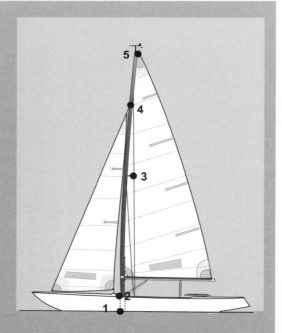

Fig 13 Mast pre-bend.

A strong pull on the mainsheet and smartly falling off to start a surf.

STEERING ON WAVES

Steering upwind also depends on the weight of the boat and shape of the front of the hull under the waterline. For example, a boat with a flat hull below the waterline (such as a Vaurien, or some offshore racing sailboats) or with a long bow overhang (like the Dragon, or classic metre-class boats) tends to slam more easily in waves. This may be countered by slightly bearing away when you are balanced on the crest and just about to drop into the trough, as the boat will heel and land on a more rounded section of the hull. This can significantly reduce slamming. Immediately after landing you can steer back up and reduce the heel, until you are about to drop into the next trough. It is also important to keep the ends of the boat as light as possible (within the class rules), so the bow and stern can be more easily lifted by the waves, making the boat pitch more efficiently through the waves. A boat with a sharp bow and a deep or V-form hull forward is less prone to slamming, and is easier to steer through waves. It is less effort to steer a straight course, with the added benefit of less slamming in the troughs.

While running downwind, there is also much to be gained when steering over the waves. The trick is to slightly head up as a wave comes up from astern, and bring the crew weight further forward so that the wave can more easily lift the stern. At just the right moment, when atop the wave and looking at the trough ahead, bear away relatively sharply and slide down the wave (surfing) while moving the crew weight further aft. When surfing you can steer very deep, and you benefit from a deeper line. Just before you are about to drive into the wave ahead, steer up and try to continue surfing on the remnants of the wave to windward. It is the responsibility of the helmsman to focus on the bottom of the wave trough, and when it is reached he must steer up again to prevent running into the wave ahead and making a Chinese gybe.

Further benefit can be gained through close coordination between the helm and the crew. For example, sharply hauling in the mainsheet and spinnaker sheets at just the

Surfing on a wake.

right moment, as the wave is crested and the boat begins to bear away, will provide additional acceleration and can make the difference between a short or a prolonged surf.

TAKING ADVANTAGE OF A WAKE

Something completely different is to take advantage of the wake of a larger (non-planing) boat. This is frequently possible in offshore yacht races under a rating system, but also in races with multiple one-design classes where the classes are not on separate courses.

For example, a 32-foot boat can take advantage of the wake of a faster 39-footer, a 39-foot boat can use the wake of a 45-footer, and so forth. In mixed one-design classes, a Vaurien or Flying Fifteen can benefit from the wake of a Dragon, while a Dragon can use the wake of an 8-metre class boat. This is possible on a beam reach, as well as on a broad reach or running downwind. On a flat downwind run the bigger boat will usually not be too happy with a smaller boat riding its wake due to partial blockage of its wind, but this tends to be more an issue in the mind

of the bigger boat's helmsman rather than based on reality. If the smaller boat is lined up with his transom and not slightly above him, it does not meaningfully block his wind. It is also absolutely legal.

So what is the trick? The bigger boat generates a wake – really a series of stern waves – due to its displacement. If you can guide your smaller boat on to its first stern wave (the wave immediately behind its transom), you can remain surfing on the wave at the same speed as the bigger boat, so long as there is not too big a difference in speed between the bigger and smaller boat (less than 1–2 knots). You can maintain this position for hours. Every time you surf over the wave toward the transom ahead it feels like you will hit their transom, but in practice this doesn't really happen because you will be held off by the wave front rising up at their transom.

There is an art to picking up the first stern wave of a bigger boat. You first need to sail higher when the bigger boat is nearing you from behind, so that the bigger boat will pass you to leeward and not to windward. Just as

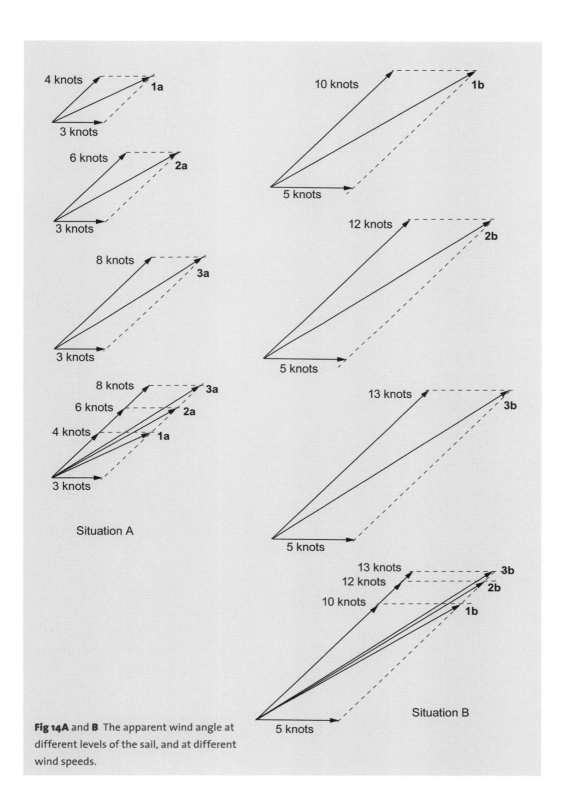

4 knots · 3 knots · **1a**

6 knots · 3 knots · **2a**

8 knots · 3 knots · **3a**

8 knots · **3a**
6 knots · **2a**
4 knots · **1a**
3 knots

Situation A

10 knots · 5 knots · **1b**

12 knots · 5 knots · **2b**

13 knots · 5 knots · **3b**

13 knots · **3b**
12 knots · **2b**
10 knots · **1b**
5 knots

Situation B

Fig 14A and **B** The apparent wind angle at different levels of the sail, and at different wind speeds.

soon as you are certain the bigger boat will do this, bear away toward him so that he passes very closely to lee. You can then bear away further when your bow is less than half a metre from the corner of his transom, and then steer immediately behind him and ride his first stern wave.

As you surf down his wave, try to resist the urge to steer past one side of his transom, because you'll lose the first stern wave before you know it. You'll end up on the second stern wave and that is less beneficial; you'll be unable to hold it for very long. You'll next end up on the third stern wave, where you may be able to get in one surf before it is all over.

If you do it really well, on a half-hour leg you can gain a half mile or more. The only requirements: get into a good starting position if a bigger boat is approaching, don't be scared, and steer precisely.

What also helps on chop is to allow some forestay sag, which in turn slackens the

THE DILEMMA FOR THE SAILMAKER AND GENOA TRIMMER

There is yet another consideration concerning the jib or genoa. The standard rule is that in light conditions the foresail needs to be fuller – but does the bottom of the foresail also need to be trimmed to be fuller (more rounded)? In this case, vector calculations can again be important.

Suppose we are sailing in light conditions and calm water. At half a metre above the waterline the wind speed is 4 knots, 2 metres above it is 6 knots, and at the top of the genoa it is 8 knots. The boat speed in this wind is 3 knots. What is the apparent wind angle for the genoa at deck height, halfway to the top, and at the top (see Fig 14, Case A)?

We see an apparent wind angle that is further forward at deck height, so the angle of attack for the foresail also needs to be sharper (tighter). The apparent wind angle is wider at 2 metres height and even wider at the top. In other words, the bottom of the foresail needs to be flatter or we need to sheet the sail further inboard by moving the fairlead further inboard. This obviously also applies to the mainsail, though to a slightly lesser extent. In light conditions and flat water we can bring the traveller up to windward and slightly ease the mainsheet, as compared to how we trim in chop. Moreover, that is also a reason we do not excessively slacken the mainsail foot on the boom.

Now we are sailing in low chop (roughly 30–50cm wave height). At half a metre above the waterline the wind speed is 10 knots, 2 metres above it is 12 knots, and at the top of the genoa it is 13 knots (see Fig 14, Case B). The boat speed in this wind is now 5 knots. The apparent wind angle at each height is almost the same. Therefore, the bottom of the sail can be fuller, which will help drive through the short chop. The conclusion is obvious: depending on the apparent wind angle, the bottom of the jib/genoa needs to be flatter or fuller.

Simply put, on flat water you flatten the bottom of a light wind genoa, and in chop you trim the bottom of a medium genoa to be somewhat fuller. This brings me back to an earlier point: you can trim a good all-around genoa or jib as required, without having to change sails.

Perfect boat handling over big waves crossing on the forward quarter.

jib/genoa luff. You can achieve this by easing the backstay or runners or loosening the shrouds (if the latter are attached to the deck aft of the mast). This will make the forward section of the jib/genoa fuller, and it will be more 'forgiving' with regard to small steering errors. In reality it is incredibly difficult, if not impossible, to hold a precise course upwind in chop. By making the front of the jib/genoa fuller you will not luff most of the sail area if you point a few degrees too high, and will only kill drive from a small forward part of the sail.

Another rule of thumb for most boats is that the trim for chop, as compared to flat water (with regards to mast bend, position of traveller, genoa leads and barber haulers – but not the forestay tension and jib/genoa luff tension), should be set as if the wind were 1–2 points higher on the Beaufort scale. Thus Force 5–6 on flat water is the same with respect to trim as Force 4 in chop.

You will need to trim a heavy boat differently from a relatively light centreboard boat or catamaran. The ideal sail profiles are also different. As a general rule, the faster the boat, the flatter the sails need to be. Additionally, on a relatively wide boat with a lot of beam carried forward (for example, a racing barge) the foresail needs to be more rounded and sheeted further outboard compared to a narrow racing yacht like the classic 6- or 8-metre, or Dragon.

Too much theory? No, it only comes down to a few things:

▶ Become comfortable with vector calculations.

▶ Embrace a logical way of thinking.

▶ Continually set, and when necessary, adjust priorities.

meteorology

WHETHER YOU LIKE IT OR NOT, TO RACE WELL YOU'LL NEED A STRONG UNDERSTANDING OF METEOROLOGY. I AM REFERRING ESPECIALLY TO THE WIND – WHY IT DROPS AND BUILDS, AND WHICH DIRECTION IT WILL TURN. OF COURSE THERE ARE WEATHER FORECASTS FROM A RANGE OF INTERNET SITES, BUT I ALWAYS LAUGH WHEN I SEE EVERYONE BEFORE A RACE BUSILY STUDYING SITES LIKE WINDGURU, PREDICTWIND AND WINDFINDER. THESE ARE NOTHING MORE THAN COMPUTER MODELS THAT PROVIDE THE PROBABLE WIND SPEEDS AND DIRECTIONS EACH HOUR.

A real danger is that the racing sailor will assume, for example, that at 11am the wind will be 6 knots coming from 190 degrees, and at 12 noon will be 9 knots at 210 degrees. If you use this to determine which side of the course to take in a windward-leeward race, then you are making a mistake. A leg takes 15 to 25 minutes, and you'd be very lucky if the wind shift occurs 7.5 to 12.5 minutes after the start.

Further, the information provided by the site does not consider shore effects, a rain cloud or thermal effects. What is most important is to think for yourself and use reasoning and logic to determine what will occur next. You will have a general picture if a weather forecast predicts that each hour the wind will shift 10 to 15 degrees to the right and increase 1 to 2 knots, but that is all you have. At most you can count on turning further right on each beat, if you have no other information. What follows are the other types of information you can gather yourself on each tack and leg of the course, no matter how long or short.

To get started, there are four causes of wind and changes in wind direction:

▶ Areas of high and low pressure

▶ Thermals

▶ The rotation of the Earth

▶ Current

For convenience I'll proceed as if you are in the Northern hemisphere. For the Southern hemisphere, virtually everything works in the opposite direction.

About high and low pressure areas: you can have an area spanning 1,000km, but also one that is a few hundred metres across. Looking at a high pressure area from above, the wind rotates to the right, or clockwise. The high pressure area can cover a large area on the weather map, but sometimes it is nothing more than a small, white cumulus cloud. A low pressure area can also cover a large area on the weather map, but it can also arrive as a dark cloud, or with a rain shower or thunderstorm. Looking at a low pressure area from above in the Northern hemisphere, the wind rotates toward the left, or anti-clockwise (Fig 15A). A common misconception is that the wind is caused by air moving

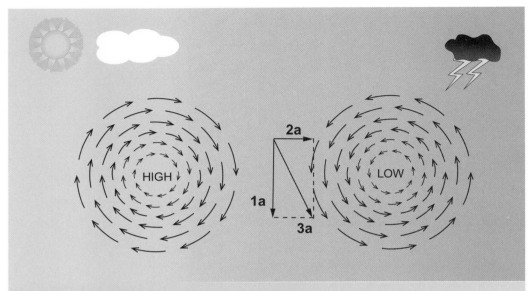

Fig 15 A The rotation of high and low pressure areas: **1** the wind direction at a height of 1,000 to 1,500m; **2** the wind component at the surface of the Earth due to the rotation of the Earth; **3** the wind direction just above the surface.

straight from a high pressure to a low, but in fact the wind passes between the high and low pressure and due to the Earth's rotation it is shifted to the left (anti-clockwise) in the Northern hemisphere.

The closer the low and high pressure areas, the closer the 'isobars' (lines of equal pressure) and the higher the wind speed.

By looking at the movement of a high or low pressure area (or both) on a weather map, we can determine how the wind direction will shift (Fig 15B).

Because warm air rises (think of a hot-air balloon) and cool air sinks, thermals are created. Warm dry sand, asphalt or paving stones warm up more quickly than water. That is why in spring and early summer thermal breezes frequently develop in the area between land and water. You can see this along the coast, in the form of a strip of white cumulus clouds just above the coastline. As the warm air over land rises, water vapour condenses as the air cools. This rising air draws in the cooler air from above the water, which in turn is warmed up over the land. The cool air moving inshore draws the warmer layer of air above it offshore, and as it cools it descends toward the surface. In this manner the air makes a full circle (Fig 16).

Effect of the Earth's rotation: Every 24 hours the Earth rotates 360 degrees around its axis, which corresponds to a distance of 40,000km at the Equator and 0 km at the poles. This has an effect on the atmosphere due to resistance from mountains, trees, houses etc and a layer of air is carried along, but if the surface is less uneven (as over water) the adjacent layer of air is carried along to a lesser degree. This has an effect on the direction and speed of the wind on the Earth's surface. I'll return to this under such topics as 'Shore Effect', the rotation of the wind along with the sun, and elsewhere.

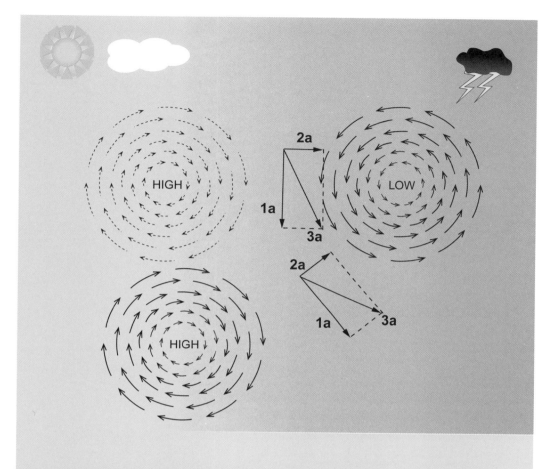

Fig 15 B Changing of the wind direction due to the displacement of a high or low pressure area.

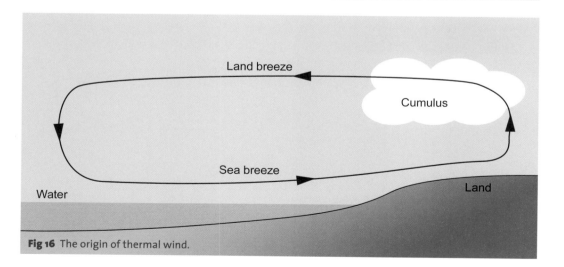

Fig 16 The origin of thermal wind.

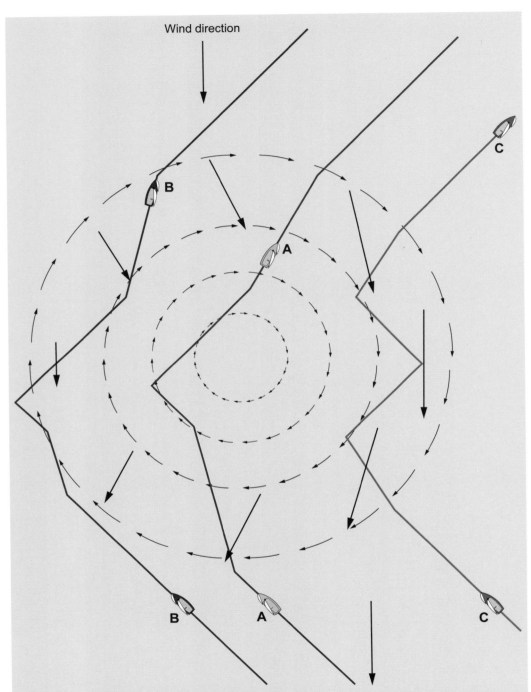

Wind direction

Fig 17 Three ways to pass a high pressure area. Of course, this is just a crude representation and the wind rotates more gradually when you approach it. In reality the course lines will not be straight lines with kinks, but instead will bend.

HIGH AND LOW PRESSURE AREAS

Example: Tacking upwind, we approach a localised high pressure area in the form of a cumulus cloud. We have three options: (a) sail directly under it, (b) pass on the left side, or (c) pass on the right side (Fig 17).

In case (a), we only benefit from some higher wind and beneficial shifts as we enter and leave the high pressure area. When completely under the cloud (that is, in the high pressure area) we will have less wind – that is where the air is rising up.

In case (b), we benefit from the wind rotating toward the right in the beginning of the passage and toward the left in the second half. During the middle of the passage, though, we have less wind, because on the left side of the high pressure area, the rightward (clockwise) rotation of air runs opposite the prevailing wind.

In case (c), through our tacks we can take advantage of the wind veering first to one side of the prevailing wind, and then to the other side. We profit further from strengthened wind during the middle of the passage, as the rotational wind reinforces the prevailing wind.

Conclusion: Approach a high pressure area on starboard tack and pass it on the right side. For a localised low pressure area, such as a rain shower, do the complete opposite: approach on port tack and pass it on the left side.

Finally, there is another factor: current. Everything that moves with a current experiences a wind of equal strength and opposite in direction to the current. I'll cover this in the next chapter.

Now that we understand the underlying causes of wind and why it changes direction, we will look at how to use this knowledge to predict the wind on a broad basis as well as on a very small scale, and take advantage of it during races.

THE EARTH'S ROTATION

Here too we can gain something. As we saw earlier in Fig 15, the rotation of the Earth adds a leftward component to the air just above the surface. This is evidenced when we see a cloud at 1,000 to 1,500 metres altitude moving at 180 degrees, but at the same time the wind on the water where we are sailing is from 155 degrees. Therefore, by observing the direction of the clouds we cannot conclude that the wind on the surface will shift to 180 degrees.

We also note that a sea breeze, caused by thermals, will rotate toward the right over the course of the day owing to the rotation of the Earth – more so the closer to the Equator we move, and less so if we move closer to the North (or South) Pole. This is logical, because the speed of the Earth relative to the atmosphere around it decreases as you approach the poles.

If, for example, the sea breeze rotates 110 degrees to the right over the course of the day in the Mediterranean, then it rotates perhaps 60 to 70 degrees in the North Sea, and along the coast of Norway maybe 30 degrees.

Conclusion: Other factors aside, when a thermal sea breeze develops, tack on the right side of the breeze as soon as you are in it.

Just as there is a difference in wind direction between a point 1,000 to 1,500 metres above

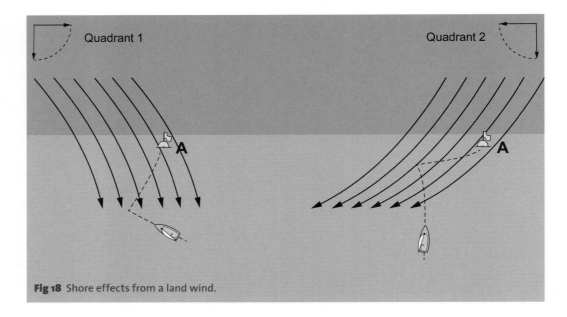

Fig 18 Shore effects from a land wind.

the surface and a point on the surface due to the Earth's rotation, there is also a difference in wind direction between wind passing over an uneven surface versus a smooth area. This is the so-called 'land effect' (sometimes referred to as coast effect or shore effect) that we frequently encounter (see Fig 18). As a land breeze passes over water (a smoother surface than the land), it will bend toward the right (clockwise). This bending is strongest in the first couple of hundred metres from the shoreline (especially if it is a rugged or built-up coast) and gradually diminishes until a few kilometres out to sea.

If the wind is angled from the left to the shore to perpendicular (Quadrant 1), after the start it is best to continue on starboard tack while there is less influence of the rotation (wind bend to the left) of the offshore wind, and then tack earlier to port. The increasing influence of the rotation as you approach the shore will lift you to the mark.

If the wind is coming from perpendicular to the shore to an angle of 90 degrees from the right (Quadrant 2), then starting on starboard

tack and sailing more directly toward the shore is again advantageous; it will bring you as quickly as possible toward the shore, where the wind comes more from the left (due to more influence of the rotation on a less smooth surface). So after tacking to port, this effect will again lift you to the mark.

Conclusion: Apart from other factors that can influence the wind, starting on starboard tack works best in an offshore breeze, due to the land effect caused by the difference in resistance between air and land and air and water.

Sometimes we experience a very unusual effect from something quite small. In the Northern hemisphere, sailing on port tack in lighter conditions (and mainly at sea), the telltales will indicate we are sailing perfectly close-hauled while the mast top windvane shows we are sailing directly into the wind. On starboard tack the windvane will indicate we are sailing slightly off the wind, though the telltales show that we cannot sail any higher. This phenomenon is

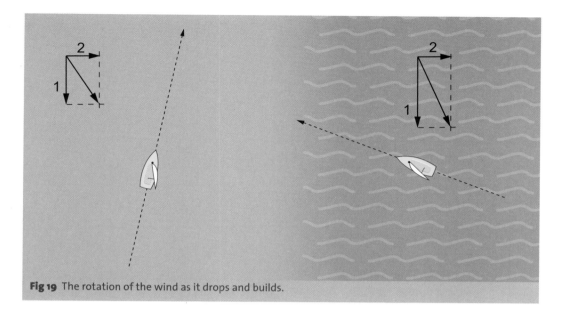

Fig 19 The rotation of the wind as it drops and builds.

called 'wind shear'. It occurs because the wind further above the water, at the height of the windvane, comes more from the right as compared to the wind that is a few metres above the not entirely flat water (which is affected more by the resistance of the surface). Should you encounter this phenomenon (mainly on boats with a mast height of 12 metres or more), then you need to trim differently on each tack. Over port make the top of the sail as closed as possible, and over starboard give the top of the sail as much twist as you can.

Finally, we have an effect that is primarily seen in very light conditions. At the moment the wind dramatically drops, the component from the Earth's rotation that bends the wind to the left (Fig 19, Vector 2) becomes greater relative to the prevailing wind (Vector 1). This causes the wind to rotate to the left. The moment that the wind builds again the wind will shift back to the right (the left component from the Earth's rotation remains the same, but is has less effect due to the stronger prevailing wind).

Conclusion: In light weather, if the wind drops regularly and you are sailing between patches of breeze, you will benefit most by getting on port tack just as soon as the wind drops, and the moment it builds again and rotates to the right you should tack back to starboard. Naturally, this applies in conjunction with all of the other factors that can influence the wind.

THERMALS

We saw how thermals develop in Fig 16. It begins with a difference in temperature between the water and the land – the water is colder than the land. This area extends further out, offshore as well as inshore. For example, if thermals begin at 11am on the coast, a few hours later the thermal wind can reach an inland lake. By the time the wind has reached the inland lake, its direction has already rotated considerably.

That is why on a beautiful spring or summer day with light weather, you can have an easterly or southerly wind on a lake 30 to 40 miles inland, but then notice dark wind

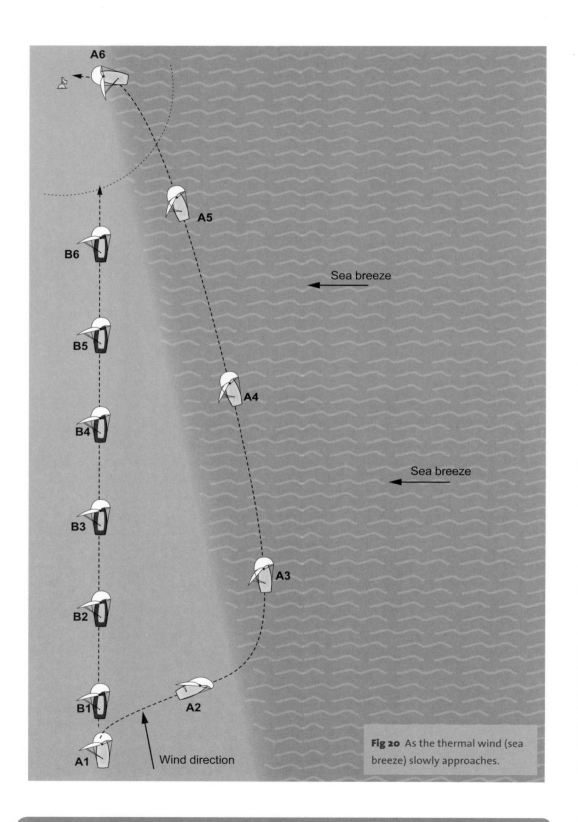

A6

A5

B6

Sea breeze

B5

B4

A4

B3

Sea breeze

B2

A3

B1

A2

A1

Wind direction

Fig 20 As the thermal wind (sea breeze) slowly approaches.

patches appearing on the water from the west-north-west or north-west (assuming the coast lies to the west).

Those who have anticipated that the thermals will arrive around this time will be sailing on the north-western side of the course, and it is not by luck that they enjoy this wind first. Further, the thermal wind doesn't approach you with the same speed as the thermal wind speed itself; no, it approaches you much more slowly. That is why it is not unusual to see a boat that is perhaps 200 to 300 metres away speed away with a big bow wave for a full five minutes before the thermal breeze reaches you. The wind speed from the thermal may be 12 to 14 knots, but it is expanding in your direction at only 2 to 3 knots (Fig 20).

Boat B sails in the most direct (shortest) line from the upwind mark to the bottom mark. Boat A has seen the thermal approaching and comes up to sail toward it. Initially A will lose position relative to B, but as soon as A reaches the stronger thermal wind it will quickly gain it back. Boat A will then have significantly better speed than B and can bear away toward the mark, and even take advantage of a shallower wind angle to the mark. This is because the thermal wind has not yet reached the layline between the top and bottom marks.

Thermals exist primarily on the coast and are called a sea breeze for good reason, but they can also arise in the area of a lake, as a street, sandy beach or car park is warmed up by the sun and becomes warmer than the lake. The difference in temperature doesn't need to be more than 3 or 4°C (5 to 8°F).

Can a sea breeze also arise if the gradient (prevailing) wind is from the land? The answer is yes! As long as the prevailing land wind remains under Force 5 it is indeed possible, and the sea breeze may even be stronger. It can somewhat amplify the sea breeze because the land wind at an altitude of 1,000 to 1,500 m in this circulating system acts as a flywheel, giving it more impulse. In other words, the air rising up from the coastline will be pushed faster back seaward, and in doing so leaves room for more rising air.

Can thermals also develop at night? Yes, that also occurs regularly, except we call it a *land breeze* instead of a *sea breeze*. It mainly occurs in late summer, when the water is still quite warm and at night the land cools off. This creates an area of land breeze over the coastline that expands toward the sea as well as inland. The air rises above the warmer water and is replaced by air from over the cooler land (land breeze). This circular air pattern is completely reversed from the sea breeze. That is why it can make sense in August and September, if the wind falls off in the evening, to consider sailing closer to the coast to take advantage of the land breeze during the evening and night.

Conclusion: If there is little or no wind and you anticipate a temperature difference between the water and the land, head toward the coast if you are currently offshore or in the middle of a lake.

The following again applies: of course, also bear in mind all of the other factors that can influence the wind.

There is also the possibility that one location can be affected by thermals from two different directions. An example of how this occurs is on the Dutch Ijsselmeer, outside of the town of Medemblik, in July and August. The situation is shown in Fig 21. This also sounds a bit odd – we always wanted to know the high and low water times on the northern (outer) side of the dyke but everyone looked at us strangely when we asked – as there are no tides on the enclosed Ijsselmeer!

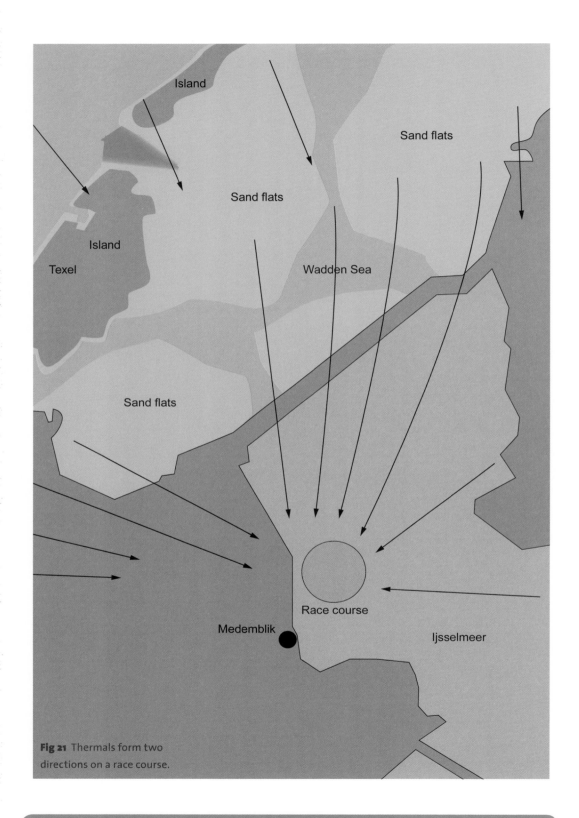

Fig 21 Thermals form two directions on a race course.

The only information we were really interested in was the low water time in the Wadden Sea, when large sandy tidal flats emerge. The sand warms quickly and can easily create a sea breeze from the north, and if it is sustained for some time, it will shift toward the north-east.

An example – around 9am there is a lovely wind from the east, 15 to 18 knots, with substantial, short waves along the lee shore by Medemblik. At the 10.30am race start the wind is still from the east at 12 knots, and around noon the wind begins to die completely. Around 1pm the sea breeze arrives at the Ijsselmeer by Medemblik, a north-west wind of around 8 knots.

In the meantime, the sandy flats north of the dyke have dried out and warmed, creating a sea breeze from the north.

Around 2 to 3pm there is a sea breeze from the North Sea coast on the left side of the course, and on the right side a sea breeze generated by the dried-out flats on the Wadden Sea. By the time it reaches the race course at Medemblik, it has shifted to the north-east. The result is that boats sailing on a port tack on the left side of the course are on the same heading as boats on a starboard tack on the right side of the course. In the middle of the course there is only a light, swirling wind.

From approximately 3 to 4pm the sea breeze out of the north-west begins to drop, while the sea breeze from the dyke shifts further east. Through the course of the afternoon this sea breeze turns further east. In the course of the evening it is combined with the land breeze from the North Sea coast, building up to 20 to 22 knots. The same pattern repeats itself the following day.

Of course, it only plays out if there are no other significant factors influencing the wind. Thus it most easily occurs in nice weather, when there is a stationary high pressure area and low water in the Wadden Sea in the early afternoon. The lesson then is: stay on the north-west side of the course in light conditions, so that you can be the first to pick up any sea breeze when it arrives. You can also benefit from the shore effect at the same time. In the course of the afternoon you should stay on the right side of the course, to take advantage of the rightward-shifting north-east sea breeze from the Wadden Sea.

The conditions above create wind as well as the rotation of the wind. I have explained how you can turn them to your advantage upwind, but of course you can equally benefit from them on downwind legs. As long as you know where the wind is and how it will fill in, you can determine in advance the preferred side of the course with regards to wind angle and strength.

If you already have the ability to predict where, when and in which direction the wind will turn, and how it will build or drop, and can apply and benefit from this, then you will understand that in the days before an important series it is wise to have a relaxed and good look at the coastline, and the land area behind it, instead of training on the water. Look especially for where the land will warm up faster due to asphalt, rocks, a south-facing rise and so forth. Swamps and marshes are not as easily warmed, and gaps between hills can bend the wind, or possibly increase the wind speed as it is forced through a gap. Also check if a river empties into the sea near the racing area, and if there is a deeper channel out to sea. Determine if you need to account for the flow of the river into the sea, or water moving back up the river. Finally, if you are sailing in tidal water ensure you know where the deeper water and the shallows lie.

Note all this on a chart and discuss it with your crew. This is truly more important than waxing your boat and sailing a practice race. You need to practise and wax your boat well beforehand, not just at the race location right before the start of the series. I always ensure that I arrive at the race location well in advance of an important series, so that I can do everything in a relaxed manner.

Now we have the practice race. In reality this is very dangerous, because it can give you a completely wrong impression of your speed as well as the characteristics of the course. Many boats cross the starting line too early in a practice race, but carry on anyway. Indeed, they want to get up to speed and not be bothered by disturbed wind from other boats, and there is no concern about an OCS.

Further, there are few boats that sail the complete race, and now and then you encounter boats on the course that left the harbour late. It means nothing to them, because it doesn't count.

There are also the characteristics of the course to consider. If at a certain time one side of the course is favoured up- or downwind, then people frequently assume it is always so and will again choose that side the next day – but not knowing *why* a certain side is better is dangerous. It may have been that way during the practice race, but perhaps that was a one-in-a-hundred exception.

I experienced this in Le Havre (France), where we won the Gold Cup, and in Kinsale

(Ireland), where we became European Champions. We had never been to either place, but arrived a week beforehand and didn't sail a single metre before the first race that counted. Instead, we properly studied the area, and on a small fishing boat we observed how the tide turned and charted the outflow of the river.

During the series this proved to be a tremendous advantage for us, and the local heroes were dumbfounded. The reason? They were accustomed to the course for the national championships that lay half a mile further down the coast, and not directly in front of the outflow from the river. Their previously preferred sides of the course were suddenly no longer advantageous, and they didn't understand why. They had become stuck in their ways and could not figure it out, which was a hefty blow to them. They didn't even finish in the top five.

Conclusion: Immerse yourself in the reason the wind does something, whether shore effect or thermals. Don't accept that 'it is always that way', but try to figure out the reasons. If not, some day you'll find yourself in the same place, or another place in different circumstances, and won't be able to figure out what you need to do on the next upwind or downwind leg.

sailboat racing in current

FIRST AND FOREMOST IT IS IMPORTANT TO UNDERSTAND WHAT EXACTLY CURRENT IS, HOW IT ACTS ON YOUR BOAT, AND ITS EFFECT ON WIND SPEED AND DIRECTION. YOU CAN COMPARE CURRENT TO SAILING ON A CONVEYOR BELT; EVERYTHING ON IT MOVES IN ONE DIRECTION, EXCEPT THINGS THAT ARE ANCHORED TO THE GROUND OR TO AN ATTACHMENT POINT BESIDE THE CONVEYOR BELT.

A funny and true story played out before the start of the Deltaweek races, near Zierikzee in Holland. In mild conditions and during spring tides the proud owner of a brand-new self-built Mini Tonner cheerfully worked his way to the starting line. Once out of the harbour he drifted back from the starting line until, as he later recounted on shore, he saw a buoy racing up the channel toward him, closing fast with a hefty bow wave, until it rammed him amidships. His boat was a complete loss and the dazed owner didn't understand what happened. He steadfastly maintained that a buoy came directly at him at high speed.

Let's now talk about the phenomenon of current, and how we can use it. To begin, current is faster in deep water and slower in shallow water – a good reason to sail out further to sea (to deeper water) when the current is with you, and more inshore (the shallows by the coastline) when it is running against you. Further, we need to understand that the current and wind are rarely aligned in the same or exactly opposite direction, and thus the wind measured at the committee boat will definitely have a different direction and speed than what we sailors measure.

Should the wind and current be perfectly aligned, in the same or directly opposite direction, then the committee boat will measure the same direction, but a different speed. Figs 22 to 25 provide several examples of the difference in wind speed and direction as seen on the committee boat and as seen by the sailors. The differences are due to the extra component – the current carrying the sailboats along. This component is opposite to the direction of the current and equal to the speed of the current.

Figs 22 and 23 show what happens when the tide turns. The committee boat measures a steady 5 knots wind, while the boats initially see 3 knots wind before the tide turns, and 7 knots afterward.

Figs 24 and 25 represent the effect of current direction on wind direction. The sailors experience an enormous change in wind direction as the tide turns, while on the committee boat the wind direction remains constant. Thus the turning of the tide, and building and slackening of the current, will change the wind direction and speed for the sailors. Those who are on the committee boat see no change in the wind direction or speed.

This is why I, as a race director, forbid taking wind measurements from the

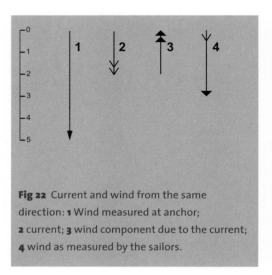

Fig 22 Current and wind from the same direction: **1** Wind measured at anchor; **2** current; **3** wind component due to the current; **4** wind as measured by the sailors.

Fig 23 Wind against current.

anchored committee boat. Instead I always have the crew on the buoy launch measure the wind speed and direction while drifting in the current; this is the only way to measure the same wind speed and direction experienced by the sailors, and to correctly lay the course and starting line.

To lay a good starting line by measuring the wind while floating along is not very difficult. What you really need to bear in mind as a race sailor is that most committees make an error when setting the top mark.

They set the mark directly upwind of the wind (that was measured while drifting), but they forget one thing: if, for example, the first upwind leg takes 45 minutes, then consider that the current will also carry you to one side during the same period – around 1.5 miles if the current is 2 knots (in Fig 26 you are pushed to the left, and in Fig 27 it pushes you to the right). Hence the race committee should place the top mark 1.5 miles further in the direction of the current, so that on each leg you will sail as long on starboard as you will on port. If the

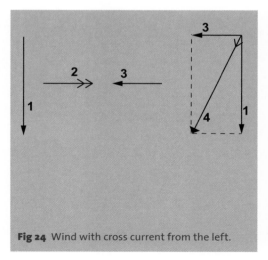

Fig 24 Wind with cross current from the left.

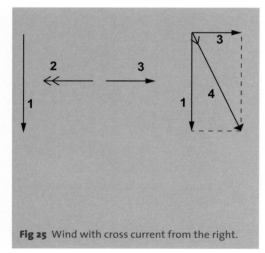

Fig 25 Wind with cross current from the right.

top mark lies directly upwind at the start, then they made a mistake. Therefore, always check before the start, after the bearing to the upwind mark is given, to see if they made a mistake. If so, take it into account so that you don't overstand the top mark!

Sailing downwind it is the same story. Further, by way of vector diagrams you can calculate the difference between the wind as measured on the committee boat and the wind measured while drifting, as well as calculate and chart the angles between the current and the wind.

Upwind as well as downwind, it is important during the last tack or gybe to the mark to have the current as much from behind as possible, and not pushing you to leeward. If we look at Fig 28, then it is best (leaving other factors aside) to start on the ship end of the line (because the cross current will push the boat toward the left, which almost always leaves room by the committee boat), and then quickly tack to port. Starting near the pin end carries significant risks: first, you don't make the line and get pushed past the pin, and second, that you have to stay on starboard tack too long, and end up overstanding the top mark. On port tack you have the current pushing you from the lee side, which gives you some lift and allows a higher line to the mark, as well as providing a higher wind speed. Should the wind drop, then you will sail an even higher line toward the mark. If you start out on starboard tack, it is difficult to determine precisely when to tack, because you do not have a clear idea of how high you will be able to sail on port tack; further, you are dead meat if the wind drops, because you'll end up too high on the buoy and will have to sail to it in less wind, against the current – and that is something you always have to avoid.

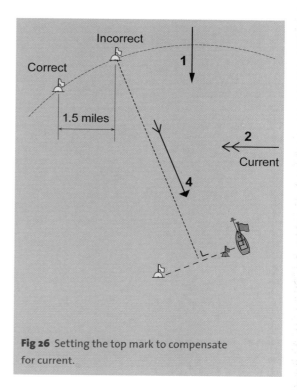

Fig 26 Setting the top mark to compensate for current.

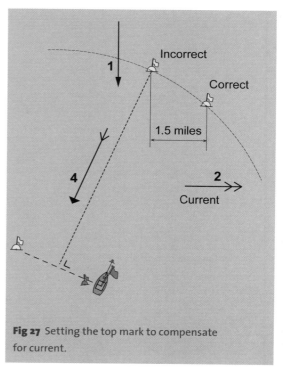

Fig 27 Setting the top mark to compensate for current.

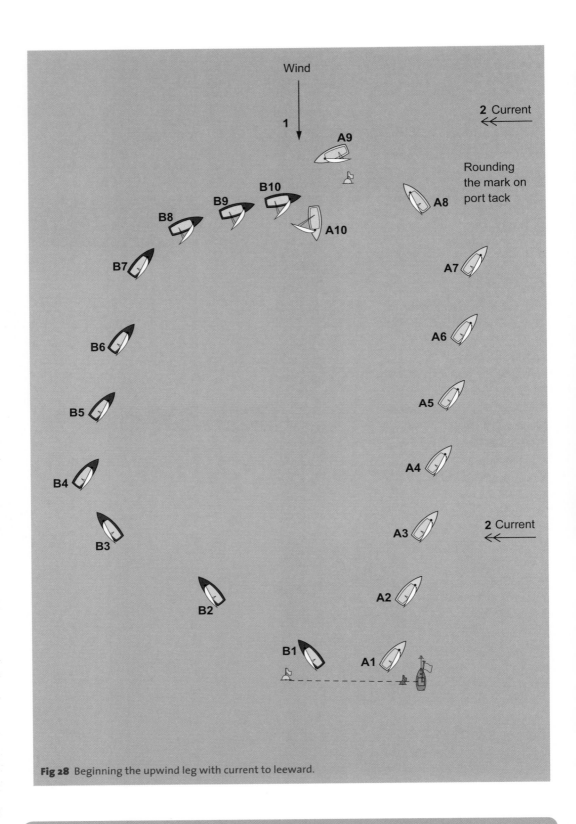

Fig 28 Beginning the upwind leg with current to leeward.

Steering just not high enough on a spreader leg with current from windward.

If after your port tack you tack back to starboard, it will not be easy to overstand the mark, as now you will be pushed a little to leeward by the current. If you don't stand the mark, no problem, you can always tack back to port comfortably below the boats that have overstood the mark on port tack and who are now fighting against the current. You'll also have the current from lee as you approach the mark and thus a higher speed over the ground than the boats sailing straight against the current from port. Often enough you see boats, having overstood the mark, hoisting spinnakers and struggling against current back to the mark.

Running downwind, it is also the intention to make the mark with the current running from behind – in this case, do a gybe-set after rounding and continue on port tack, and in the last stretch before the mark gybe back to starboard – but keep steering below the mark!

If you are in a situation where the current is running from the left across the course, then everything relating to the start and the manoeuvres is reversed. Start on the pin end (you'll be lifted and will make the pin easily)

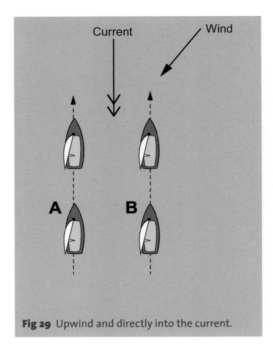

Current   Wind

A   B

Fig 29 Upwind and directly into the current.

and continue on starboard. Starting on the ship end is now dangerous, because the current will carry you toward (and perhaps past) the committee boat, and boats will try to cut back in on the ship end. Even if you manage a good start you will probably be forced to tack to port relatively early by the boats below you. The result: a good chance you will sail too long on port tack and overstand the mark, because after you tack to starboard, the current will push you higher.

Coming to the top mark on port tack isn't a real problem, because you can tack under the boats on starboard tack. If at the last moment you're not going to make the mark, you can ease the sheets and luff up to wind, let the current carry you sufficiently past the mark, and then bear away and sail clear of it. It is in fact highly recommended in this situation on port tack, because working against the tide on starboard tack costs a lot more. Further, it is now best after the rounding to sail close to the wind on

starboard, and not to gybe until you are close to the bottom mark.

The following figures show situations that are frequently encountered in current. In Fig 29 we see two boats (A and B), both sailing directly into the current on starboard tack. In Fig 30 boat B steers slightly higher (though still very much against the current). The result is that with the same or somewhat higher speed his course is significantly higher than A. We see the reason in Fig 32. If we resolve the current vector into two component vectors, one parallel to the centreline of the boat (I) and one perpendicular to the course (II), the component perpendicular to the centreline will push the boat higher (to windward). This also causes a new wind component (III); when combined with the wind that A and B both experience, the resulting wind (IV) comes at a more open angle and is stronger, which allows B to steer a bit higher.

In Figs 31 and 33 we see what happens if A steers slightly lower; the wind weakens and the angle becomes tighter. In either case the helmsman may think there is something wrong with the trim, but that is absolutely not the reason. The real question is: do you get the current a little from windward or leeward? Remember that just 1 or 2 degrees in light wind is enough to see a substantial difference.

Around the turning of the tide there are two things to know to benefit from it, namely (a) when the tide turns (slack water) and (b) where it first turns – inshore or offshore. Unfortunately, you will not find this in the tide tables; they only provide the high and low water times. The turning of the tide frequently occurs hours before or after high or low water. Of course, for this you can refer to tidal charts, so do not confuse the two. Further, the tide can turn earlier or later if

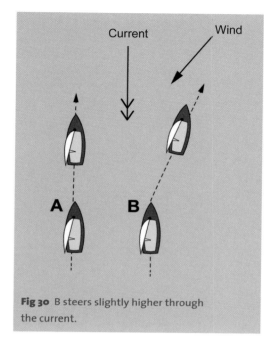

Fig 30 B steers slightly higher through the current.

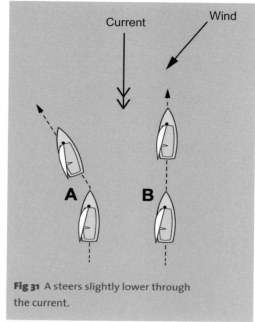

Fig 31 A steers slightly lower through the current.

there is (or has been) a strong wind against the tide, or in the same direction. How do you recognise the tide turning? Frequently there is a narrow strip across the water, sometimes only 5 to 10 metres wide and comprising seaweed, algae and foam, where the pattern of the sea is different on each side. For example, the water is flatter on the side where the wind is in the same direction as the current, while the side where the wind is against is lumpier, with short and steep little waves. You may have heard that there is little current in the area just on either side of the line. That really doesn't make sense; the water layers do not have any mutual resistance, and there is indeed current along this line – sometimes even stronger than further away from the line.

In Fig 34 we see what you should do if two tides are running across the course (rising

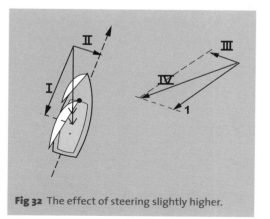

Fig 32 The effect of steering slightly higher.

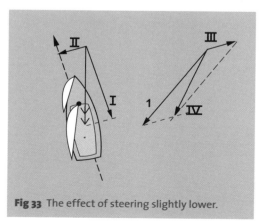

Fig 33 The effect of steering slightly lower.

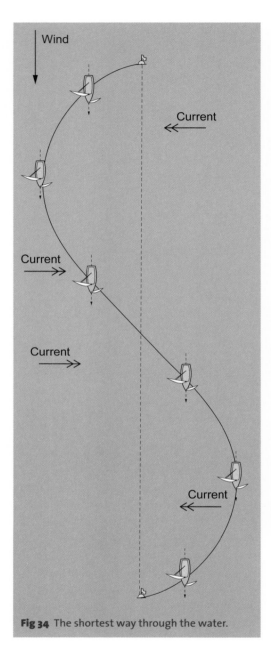

Fig 34 The shortest way through the water.

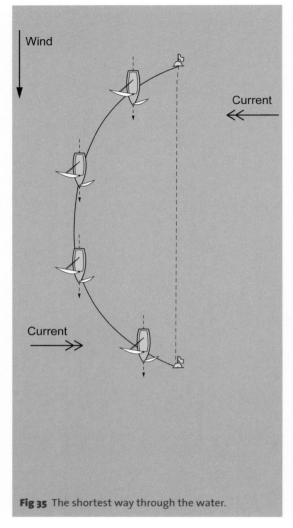

Fig 35 The shortest way through the water.

Fig 35 shows the same thing over one tide, where the tide turns in the middle of the leg, with the shortest path through the water and the resulting path over ground. Always bear in mind that you are sailing a sine shape or an arc over the ground – especially with regards to shallows and so forth!

All variations, such as if the leg is shorter or longer, are easy to calculate. An example is given in Fig 36, where the leg is over a tide and a half. If you sail directly and without correction you will end up at point A instead

and falling), precisely along a line drawn between the two marks. In this case, you just steer directly from one mark to the other. Through the water you steer the shortest course, a straight line; however, over the ground you will follow a sinusoidal path.

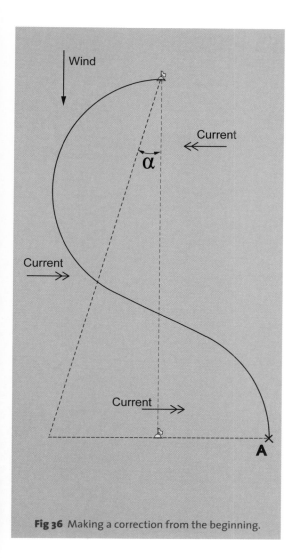

Fig 36 Making a correction from the beginning.

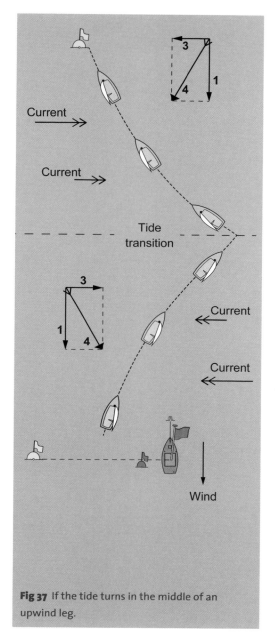

Fig 37 If the tide turns in the middle of an upwind leg.

of at the mark. To follow the shortest, thus straight line through the water, you need to first correct your course from the first mark to the second by angle alpha.

If the tide runs more or less perpendicular to the wind direction, and turns during the leg, make your first tack with the current running from leeward. The following advice applies even more strongly – beware that you do not overstand the mark! As the tide turns (as in Fig 37), the wind will shift toward the right. If instead the current comes from the

left at the start and then after slack water comes from the right, then the opposite applies: first make a starboard tack, and around slack water go to port tack. Around the time the tide turns, the wind will turn toward the left (refer again to Figs 24, 25 and 28).

Fig 38 depicts the ideal course to follow, on a race course where the current is perpendicular to the line to the first mark and the tide turns during the race. Let us first assume the following:

▶ The wind is from the west and the course to the first mark does not need to be corrected, because the tide is turning in the middle of the course.

▶ The current is from the south, and after the tide turns it comes from the north.

▶ The tide turns first by the coast; the transition line between the rising and falling tides moves progressively out to sea (shown as line A at the start of the race, then B, and line C around the end of the race).

We start on starboard tack on the committee boat end, with the current coming from leeward, until we reach the tide transition line, and just before reaching it we tack to port (point 1). We continue on port tack parallel to the transition line to point 2, where we tack back to starboard to make the top mark. Here we need to pay attention, because while we could sail a little higher on port tack, as we sail into and cross the transition line A we will need to bear away slightly as the wind component from the current changes direction. Further, we need to pick point 2 for the tack back to the mark so that even with the wind shifting left and the tide pushing us from windward, we still have room to make the mark.

Immediately after rounding the top mark we gybe and begin the downwind leg on port tack, until we arrive at the tide transition at point 4 (which in the meantime has shifted further to sea). At point 4 we gybe to starboard and sail parallel to the transition line A, to point 5. We choose point 5 so that

when we gybe back to port, we have wind off the quarter and can steer under the bottom mark. If we gybe too early and try to sail dead downwind to the bottom mark, there is a huge chance that we'll end up above the mark, and will then have to gybe back to starboard and run against the current – which would be disastrous.

After the bottom mark we sail upwind on starboard tack to point 6, where we again come to the tide transition line. Here we will tack to port and run along the line to point 7, where we tack back to starboard and head to the upwind mark for the second time. Rounding the buoy we immediately gybe and head on port to point 9, at the tide transition line (which has again shifted further to sea). Here we gybe to starboard and sail along the right side of the transition line to point 10 (where the same conditions apply as for point 5 in the earlier downwind leg). At this point we gybe to port, and we approach the mark from below with a wide wind angle.

Immediately after rounding the mark (point 11) we proceed on starboard tack and look for the transition line (now further out to sea, at position C). Immediately before the line we tack to port (point 12) and sail close to the right side of the line to point 13, where we then tack back to starboard and head directly to the finish line. In summary, understand the current expected during a race, anticipate changes, and be observant!

Fig 39 is how an ideal race course would look if there were current across the course. Ideal in the sense that on the upwind legs the sailors are on starboard tack for as long as they are on port tack, and they need to gybe on the downwind legs. Frequently, this is the question in laying a course with a cross current: compensate for it on the upwind leg, or on the downwind leg? There is only one good answer – both! I can understand that for

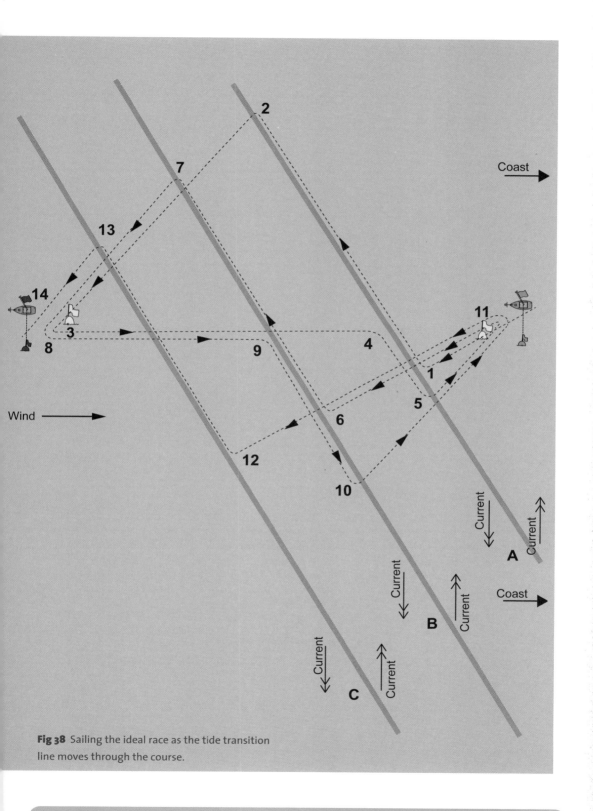

Fig 38 Sailing the ideal race as the tide transition line moves through the course.

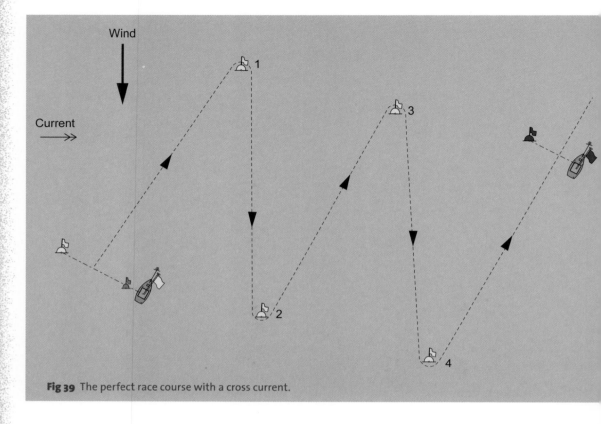

Fig 39 The perfect race course with a cross current.

a club race or other less important races it is not always possible to lay every buoy in each leg so that you have the perfect accordion-course, as in Fig 39. A good alternative is to position the top (1) and bottom (2) buoys to compensate for the cross current, but add a short beam reach from the bottom buoy to a third buoy (3) behind the starting line (Fig 40). With this layout, boats can also finish on the reach, across a line between the committee boat and a finish buoy (4).

The big advantage is the whole course can remain in place, including the committee boat, and you can start the next race very quickly. The only other consideration is that when the cross current is from the left (as seen in the direction of the top buoy from the starting line), the marks must be rounded to starboard, and if it is from the right the marks must be rounded to port. This is not really a problem per se, it is only a question of hoisting a red or a green flag on the committee boat.

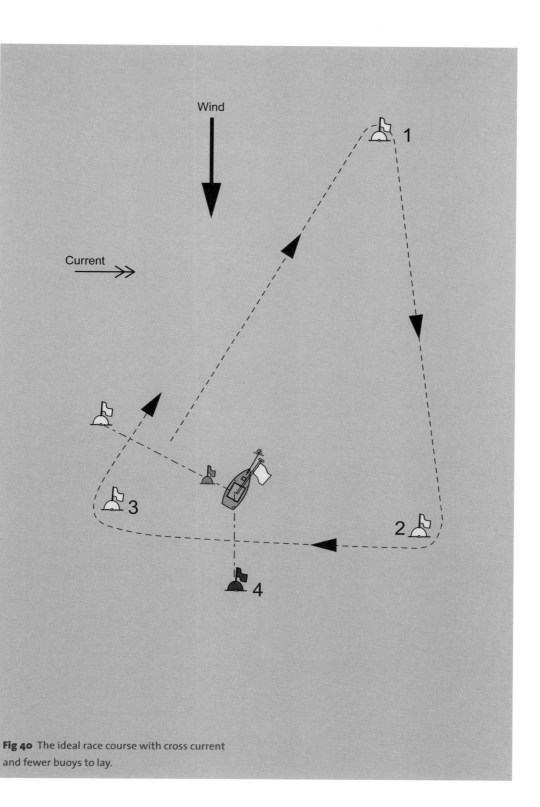

Wind

Current

1

2

3

4

Fig 40 The ideal race course with cross current and fewer buoys to lay.

chapter 10

tactics

OBVIOUSLY IT IS IMPOSSIBLE HERE TO COVER EVERY TACTICAL SITUATION THAT CAN ARISE IN A SAIL RACE. SO INSTEAD I'LL PROVIDE A FEW ILLUSTRATIVE EXAMPLES, TO HELP YOU DEVELOP A LOGICAL WAY OF THINKING SO THAT YOU CAN RECOGNISE A SITUATION BEFOREHAND, AND DETERMINE YOUR REACTION IN ADVANCE.

In essence, we can divide tactics into three elements:

1. Tactics in relation to other boats
2. Tactics with respect to the race rules
3. Tactics with respect to the wind

One of the most important points to remember for your tactics is that the wind always acts like a sine wave – make use of this fact. The time between the maximum shift to the left and maximum to the right can vary from 1 or 2 minutes to 20 minutes, and the variation from right to left can range from a few degrees to as much as 20 or 30 degrees. That is why it is important before the start to determine the amount of time (period) and number of degrees between the shifts from left to right, in the absence of other influences. Sail a part of the windward leg several times before the start to determine this, and write it down.

TACTICS WITH RESPECT TO OTHER BOATS

Among other things, this depends on if there is only one race, or if there is a series of races. If it is just one race you can take a few more risks. If you are trying to win a series, bear in mind that few series are won with all first-place finishes, while on the other hand series are relatively often won without a single first place – but you need finishes in the top 5, or even top 10. In other words, make sure you stay with the top 10, and don't take too many risks. If in a fleet of 80 or 100 boats you are rounding the top mark in the top 10, and you work to gain a few places during the race, then there is a good chance you can win the series.

Before I offer examples relating to tactics, I first want to bring up the rule that is the most sinned against – and that is the full-throated 'Starboard!' someone yells at a boat to port. In eight out of ten cases this is a stupid bit of machismo, rather than necessitated by a tactical insight. After all, you are on starboard tack for a reason, and you want to stay on this tack!

The usual outcome of this shout is that your opponent on port looks under his boom, then waits as long as possible before he decides to tack close below you. Due to the same macho behaviour he may forget why he is on port tack and refuse to pass behind you. The result is that within a short span of time you are in the disturbed air of the boat below you, and you have to tack to port – something you really didn't want to do, otherwise you would have tacked earlier. You can make things worse by pinching up at the last minute, so that your opponent recognises

Yes, you have right of way on starboard. But will it make you happy if someone turns so closely under you?

Letting a boat on port tack pass ahead has the advantage of letting you continue on starboard.

he cannot pass ahead – but now you have lost your speed at the very moment he turns alongside you!

So instead it is a good time to assess if he is going to cause you problems if he turns. If so, bear away slightly and take the speed, and wave to him to pass ahead. Let him clearly see that he may (and can) pass clearly ahead of you. If he doesn't, at least you have speed and the ability to sail higher if he nevertheless decides to tack. If you are the port tack boat and see that you cannot quite pass ahead, it is helpful to ask if you can pass ahead. Calling 'OK?' is sufficient. Among top international sailors, most of the time you will immediately see a hand waving you across, or hear a response of 'OK' or 'Go ahead'.

Whether to attack or defend depends on your position in the overall standings. Naturally, you will take more risks if you fall further in the standings as the series progresses, in part depending on whether you have already used your discard race. To defend on the upwind leg it is important whether you turn below, ahead, or above your opponent. You can always tack to put your opponent in your foul air, but that only makes sense in exceptional circumstances. Your opponent will turn away again and again, and the usual result is that both of you will be reeled in by the trailing fleet. Make your tack so that you let your opponent 'live', or in other words, grant him clear air. Where you tack in relation to your opponent depends on where you are in the sine wave of the wind direction.

An example is shown in Fig 41. In this drawing Boat B tacks to port, but Boat A knows the wind will again shift to the right, and therefore tacks ahead and slightly below B. The result is that B sails behind A and automatically tries to sail higher to stay in clear air, which costs him some distance to A.

If the other boat can't tack away because they are on the layline, then giving them foul air can add to your lead.

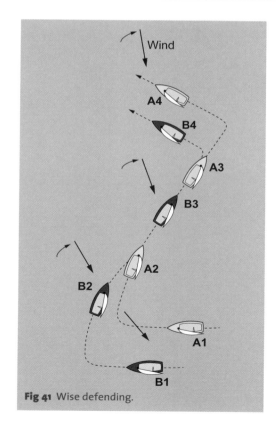

Fig 41 Wise defending.

The moment the wind shifts to the right, B finds himself in the foul air of A and will tack to starboard. Boat A tacks directly with B and will lie above him. If the wind continues to shift to the right, then B will turn inside A, and B will again be in A's foul air; B will drop further behind, and be forced into a disadvantageous port tack. If B tacks (on to the wrong tack), then A tacks right above B, so that as the wind shifts back to the left A will turn above B. B will yet again be in the foul air from A and will further lose ground to A. In this manner A slowly but surely lengthens

his lead over B without losing position relative to the rest of the fleet, because A and B are both tacking at the right time relative to the wind shifts. In short, always turn a little under your competitor if you know the wind will shift lower, and right above him if the wind is shifting higher.

If, on the other hand, you are attacking and have the misfortune of an opponent continually tacking above you so that you are stuck in his foul air, then do the following: turn at the extremes of the sine wave pattern that the wind direction is following. That is to

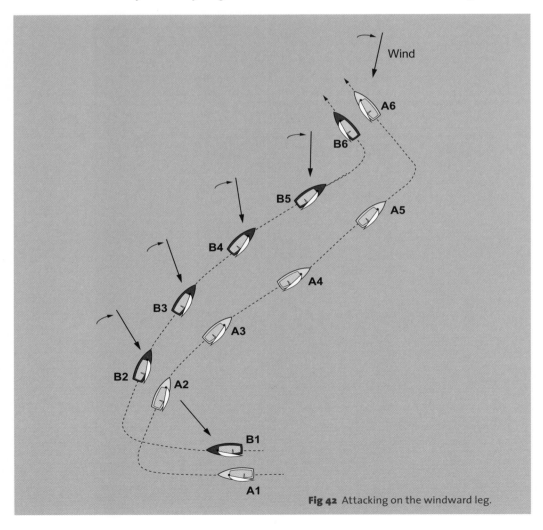

Fig 42 Attacking on the windward leg.

say, tack from starboard to port at the moment the wind is at its maximum point from the left (Fig 42) and bear away slightly. This will give you more speed and free air, and you'll arrive sooner to where the wind shifts back to the right as you'll take the inside curve. As soon as the wind has shifted to the right, tack to starboard and the game repeats itself. In this way, with each tack you come closer to forcing a starboard-port situation, which is the time to force your opponent on to the wrong tack. The most beautiful way is if you are on port tack and bear away to pass just behind him. Your opponent cannot turn at that moment and will have to stay on his tack, until he ends up above and behind you. Later you will tack back ahead of him, and you can play the game of defence as shown in Fig 41.

It is a little more difficult if you are on starboard tack, namely because you are on the good tack and he isn't. Make sure you can continue on this tack! If you aren't 100 per cent sure he will pass behind you, you have two choices: (a) you bear away slightly and clearly gesture to him to pass ahead or (b) you bear away slightly and build some speed so that if he tacks ahead and below you, you can come up a bit to create some separation between the boats and because of your higher speed you will pull ahead (Fig 43).

As you approach the top mark, be well aware of where you are on the sine wave of the changing wind direction. This will dictate whether or not you will gybe after rounding the mark. As you near the mark, remember this: do not immediately hoist your spinnaker, or ease the mast forward, or set other trim! There is a huge chance that you'll find yourself in a situation where you cannot manoeuvre to either side due to boats above and/or below you, and you will sail most of the leg in a place where you don't want to be at all.

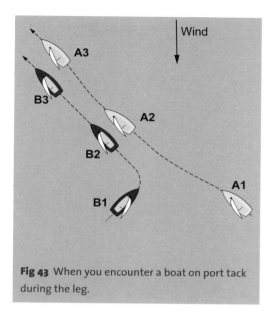

Fig 43 When you encounter a boat on port tack during the leg.

Let us first assume that the wind direction is on the right side of the sine wave (Fig 44), or in other words, is coming more from the right. In this case you want to round the mark and gybe, so you can start the downwind leg on port. First and foremost, make sure there is nobody between you and the mark, otherwise you will not be able to bear away directly and gybe. What is better is to steer up as you approach the mark and slow down. Further, ensure you leave several metres between you and the mark so that after the gybe you can sail next to the buoy, and steer a somewhat higher course so that nobody can sneak in above you. Then you can hoist the spinnaker and set the trim.

I'd like to note here that most sailors ease the foot of the mainsail a bit when running downwind. I've never really seen the benefit. In my view, while running it is a question of presenting as much surface area of the mainsail as possible (and you only make it smaller when you ease the outhaul), because there is not the need for the wind to stream along it as when sailing upwind.

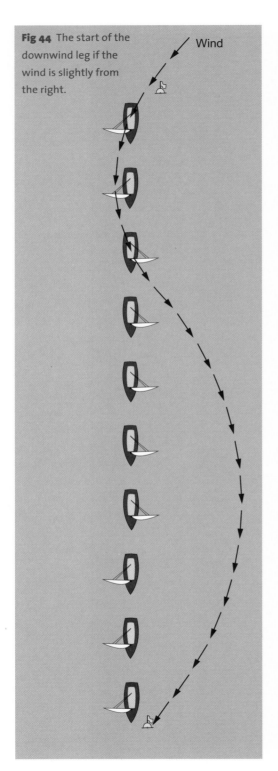

Fig 44 The start of the downwind leg if the wind is slightly from the right.

Wind

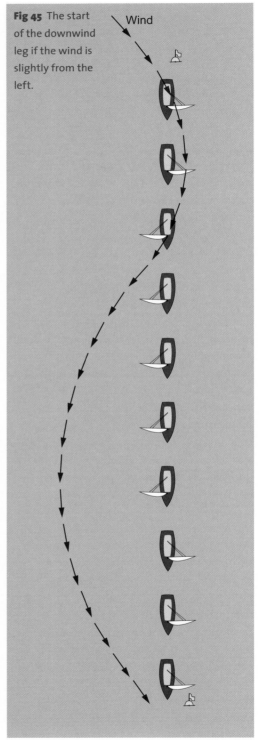

Fig 45 The start of the downwind leg if the wind is slightly from the left.

Wind

If the wind is on the left side of the sine wave (Fig 45), then you won't want to gybe after rounding the mark and instead begin the downwind leg on starboard. In this case, ensure nobody is above you as you round, and gain some height under white sails before you bear away. By doing this, you won't be blanketed by the boats behind you that bear away directly after rounding. Make it very clear from the beginning that you are going to sail high, compelling the boats behind you to immediately hoist their spinnakers and sail below you. You also avoid the boats just ahead that are busy setting their spinnaker, who otherwise may come up to the wind a little later.

What should you do after the bottom mark? First, before you get to the bottom mark check to see where you are in relation to the wind direction sine wave. If the wind is coming from the left of the sine-wave pattern, then you want to begin on port tack because the direction of the shift will lift you toward the mark. If your opponent is behind you at the bottom mark and he tacks immediately to starboard, wait a bit. There is a good chance he will shortly tack back to port because he was trying to get into clear air. The instant the wind shifts back to the right, tack back to starboard and you will have made a significant gain on him – in the meantime, he has tacked twice, and was turning outside of you while the wind shifted (see Fig 46).

If the wind is from the right of the sine wave and you hold a comfortable lead, tack to starboard immediately after the bottom mark. If your opponent is close behind you, continue on port tack. Most likely he will immediately tack; do not hesitate to also immediately follow him to starboard tack and bear away just a little. In doing so you'll soon put him in your foul air, and he'll be

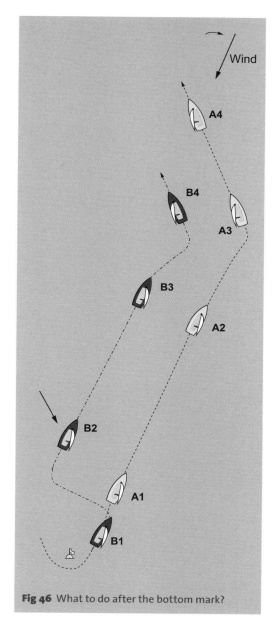

Fig 46 What to do after the bottom mark?

forced to tack back to the disadvantaged port tack. He lost enormously in the process, because he had to tack twice in close succession after rounding the bottom mark, while he sailed in the disturbed water from other boats; you gave him your foul air; and after tacking to the less favoured tack he'll

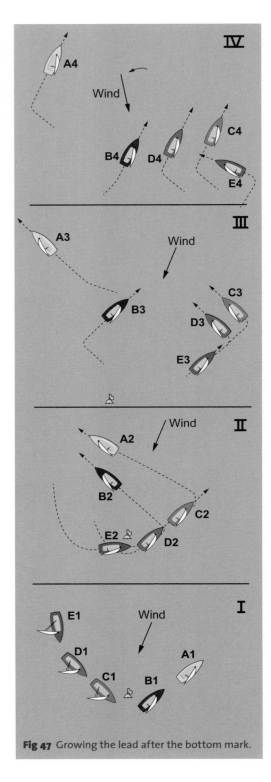

Fig 47 Growing the lead after the bottom mark.

eventually have to deal with boats that continued even further on starboard after the bottom mark (see Fig 47).

If your opponent goes behind C and D, then he gives up even more to you. Above all he is on the wrong tack and he will lose a lot as the wind shifts back to the left. If he tacks to starboard ahead of C, then he loses whatever speed was left and is completely shut down, as he will be in your foul air and later blanketed by C as he passes upwind. Even if C doesn't blanket him he has to stay in your foul air, because he cannot tack due to C. If the wind shifts to the left, then he must first wait for C to tack, and if he then tacks just above and behind C, he will need to pinch up and still deservedly ends up in the foul air from D and C. You can then turn above B, C and D, and you control the whole group. In this way you can frequently gain 50 to 80m within a few minutes, which is enough to defend easily. You have no further need to put them in your foul air and only need to keep on the right side of the others (ahead or above) with respect to the sine-wave shift in wind direction.

Making a long tack. If the course to the top mark is one long tack, followed by a short tack to the mark, always turn a little under the boats in the same long tack, whether you have room to pass easily in front of them or not. Let's suppose the long tack is on port (see Fig 48). If you turn under them, you have three options: (1) the wind shifts slightly to the left, and you can lay the mark (see Fig 48A); (2) the wind direction remains constant, you neither win nor lose; and (3) the wind shifts to the right, whereby you turn inside the other boats, who fall behind while you gain an advantage to them toward the mark after tacking (see Fig 48B).

Obviously the same applies for a long tack on starboard. In short, you can't lose. Only in

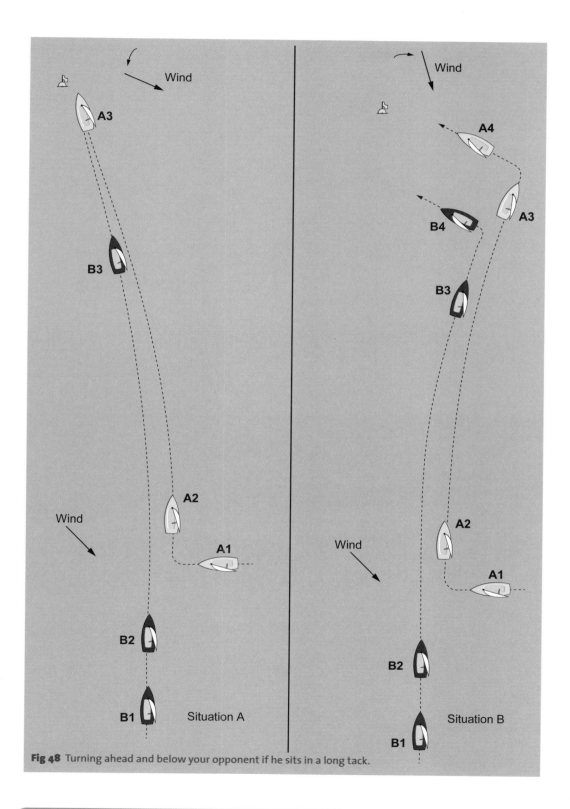

Wind

A3

B3

Wind

A2

A1

B2

B1   Situation A

Wind

A4

B4   A3

B3

Wind

A2

A1

B2

B1   Situation B

Fig 48 Turning ahead and below your opponent if he sits in a long tack.

First taking a little height without the spinnaker would have been helpful.

even further ahead. Remember the old saying – cross them if you can. A well-known sailor held first place overall in standings during the Olympics, and was leading in the final race. She wanted to increase her lead and sailed away from the fleet. The result: she ended up on the wrong side and lost the gold medal. In sailboat racing it is not how much you win by, but that you win! Whether by 5 minutes or 5 seconds, it doesn't make any difference.

The so-called 5% rule, also known as the law of Conservation of Misery. If you are not in a good position when rounding the bottom mark, there are two things you can do at the beginning of the windward leg – either continue on port tack or tack to starboard. People assume you have a 50% chance with each, but the leaders nearly always tack to the best side of the course. If you pick the other tack because you think that in one swift blow you'll make huge gains, you'll be wrong nine times out of ten. Hence you only have a 5% chance! The best advice is to continue plugging along the good tack, perhaps with a small tack to gain some height, and exploit the mistakes of others.

the last part of the leg, where both tacks become the same length and the wind still hasn't turned, should you revert to normal tactics. If you are in the lead, potentially make another small defensive tack to gain height.

If you round the mark behind a few boats but on the coming leg you are faster than the boats ahead, take a little extra height or fall off somewhat after rounding. The biggest mistake you can make is to sail directly behind an opponent until you are right on his transom. If you then try to sail over him, he will (quite rightly) begin to luff up – and trying to sail just below him usually doesn't work either. Therefore, determine beforehand what you want to do, and from early on create some height or depth.

If you start on lee, or are sailing leeward of the fleet and the wind shifts so that you can cross ahead (also if you have to pass behind one or two boats), then do it immediately. You can always tack back above the fleet. Don't instead continue on the same tack and hope the wind shifts further so that you will end up

If you are not in the lead at the end of a windward leg, at least take care that you do not join the row of boats on starboard tack that have followed the layline to the top mark for some time. Everyone in this line is pinching up to keep from dropping into the foul air from the boat immediately ahead (which frequently happens nonetheless), or boats try to join higher in the row – also called 'stacking' – to avoid this. In other words, they actually oversail the mark. It is better instead to make your starboard tack so that you end up 10 or 15 boat lengths below this line. You'll enjoy clean air while they are sailing in each other's foul air, and gaps will develop in the line. Tack to port when you are within five to eight boat

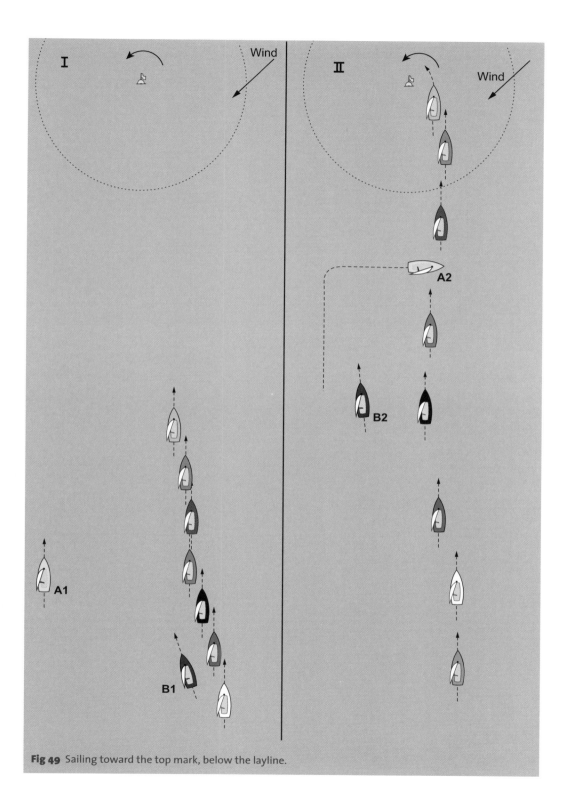

Fig 49 Sailing toward the top mark, below the layline.

If after a windward start you can cross ahead on port tack ... do not hesitate.

lengths from the mark, and then tack back into one of the gaps that has opened (Fig 49).

If you are sailing cleanly on starboard and within a few lengths of the mark and an opponent approaches on port, always steer a line slightly below the mark. He'll be forced to tack early and there is a good chance he will not make the mark (Fig 50A). If you instead continue sailing high on the wind, he will tack later and can get inside of you at the mark (Fig 50B).

Whether you attack or defend, always try to stay on the favoured side of your opponent; what constitutes the favoured side can depend on a rain shower, a high pressure area, cold front, thermals, shore effect, or an

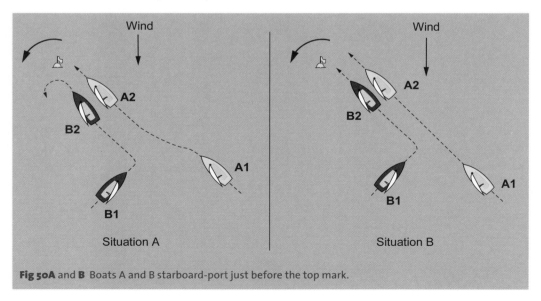

Situation A

Situation B

Fig 50A and **B** Boats A and B starboard-port just before the top mark.

anticipated wind shift in connection with the sine-wave wind pattern. Thus you want to be ahead or above your opponent if you are defending and expect to be later headed or lifted, and below or behind him if you are attacking and expect that you'll soon bear away or come up. Make some drawings and get familiar with these situations.

The second: If defending, always try to force your opponent as close to the layline as possible. At some point he has no other choice but to sail behind you to the top buoy, otherwise he will overstand the mark. You can achieve this by making sure on one tack he falls in your foul air and has to tack away, and on the other tack he has clean air (Fig 51).

Now another practical tip for boats with a spinnaker and furling jib. After rounding the top mark, always hoist your spinnaker before furling the jib. The first reason is that you can't do much when you only have the mainsail – you can't blanket someone or luff them up. Second, there is a good chance that the loose-hanging spinnaker halyard will get twisted around the jib halyard while you are furling, preventing you from hoisting the spinnaker. At the bottom mark always unfurl the jib/genoa first, take the spinnaker pole away, and then drop the spinnaker. The reason? Without the jib/genoa you'll lie near or past the buoy like a sitting duck. Further, you won't be able to accelerate during the rounding. There is also a good chance the spinnaker halyard will get turned around the jib while you are unfurling, and you'll be unable to fully unfurl it. Additionally, you won't be able to get pressure out of the spinnaker before the drop without bringing it behind the jib. Last but not least, if the spinnaker pole is still up when you round or just afterward, you cannot directly tack should that be necessary. Drop the spinnaker

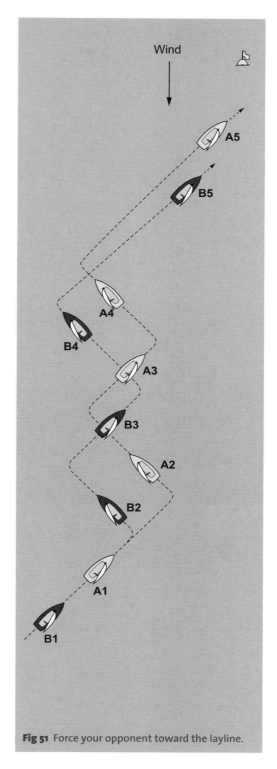

Fig 51 Force your opponent toward the layline.

The well-known 'stacking' on port near the top mark costs a lot.

enough in advance; very often you see that someone gains 1 or 2m by keeping the spinnaker up until the last moment, but after the mark loses 20 or 30m due to a poor rounding and late clean-up. The only exception to my advice here is in light air, when you are approaching the bottom mark against the current.

Another thing to remember is that if you see yourself getting drawn into a luffing match, then unfurl your jib/genoa straight away. This helps enormously in case the spinnaker collapses while you gain height.

Blanketing. Frequently people don't know how they can blanket another boat, or when they are blanketed themselves. Fig 52 is an example. Let's say the wind speed is 5m/sec (10 knots), both boats are sailing at 3m/sec (6 knots), and the distance between A and B is 20m. Boat A thinks that he is blanketing B, because he is

lying precisely along the true wind line to Boat B. In reality, the blanketing will arrive at that point 20/5=4 seconds later. At that point, B will have sailed 4×3=12 m further ahead, in position B2. If A wants to blanket opponent B, then he needs to first position himself 12m further ahead. The same applies upwind, if you want to give an opponent foul air. That is why it is helpful to sketch situations with regard to blanketing or giving foul air, so that on the water you can estimate earlier when you will blanket an opponent (or not), and when you will be blanketed yourself.

Finally, a few more points concerning the start. If at the end of the series you have only one more opponent to beat, then start right under him – the closer the better. You can often accomplish this by sailing behind him on port just before the start. When he tacks back to starboard, turn just ahead and below him. If he already has a hefty discard race and you don't, then it is worth the trouble to luff him up on the wrong side of the committee boat when it is about a minute before the start. In this case, the one-minute rule works perfectly for you; you both end up starting at the back but it makes no difference to you as you don't already have one poor race to discard.

A second possibility is to start just above and slightly ahead of your opponent, and then fall off slightly over him (or further below, but still enough ahead of him). In either case he will soon suffer from your foul air, and you can hold him there after each tack. There is, of course, a huge chance you or both of you will start too early, but in this case it is absolutely irrelevant.

If it isn't a question of having to beat one opponent in the final race of the series, then it is frequently advantageous to look for a pair of weaker opponents to start between. In

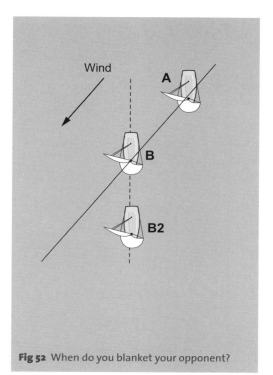

Fig 52 When do you blanket your opponent?

Small gains by leaving the spinnaker up a little longer, and a lot lost after rounding the bottom mark. This is penny wise and pound foolish.

Not yet blanketing.

doing so, it is usually easier to create some room at the place you want to start. If you do not plan to start at one end of the line or the other, it is very difficult to judge how far you are from the line (especially with a long starting line). Hence you can benefit from this little optical trick. On a starboard tack near the line and sitting on the windward side, first look over your right shoulder at the committee boat to starboard, then look at the pin end to port. You will get the impression that you are pretty much on the starting line. Now turn yourself 180 degrees around in the boat and look at the committee boat on the starboard side of the line, and over your left shoulder at the pin end mark on the port side of the line. You'll probably get the impression that you are still lying about 10 to 20 metres behind the line. As is so often the case, the truth lies in the middle.

TACTICS WITH REGARD TO THE RACING RULES

To begin with, it is absolutely essential to master the racing rules before you start racing. That doesn't mean that you just know them, but above all that you understand them. In addition to reading and compre-hending them, consider them as they relate to different possibilities and situations that may occur. Not only because otherwise you'll run into problems, but also because you can cause problems for other competitors and spoil the game for them too. The above applies not only to the helmsman, but also to the crew.

Careful reading is also incredibly important, because people often assume things that are not in them at all. What always matters is that you understand the rules regarding right of way between boats that encounter each other, as well as grasping the underlying definitions. You simply can't play games or make a sport of it if you don't understand the rules. There is yet one more thing – every four years you have to study the rules anew, because they are revised every four years, following the Olympic Games. On the one hand it is funny, and on the other hand tragic, to see how many racing sailors know everything about football rules, and sit in front of the television with pretzels and a beer second-guessing the referee. However, on the water, where they are busy competing in their own sport, they do not understand the rules. During races I still hear the call 'You have to sail to the mark', a shout about something that hasn't been in the racing rules for ages.

In the previous season, during a big series with various classes racing together on the same course, I saw a few nice examples of how not to do it. On a windward leg I was on starboard tack and a boat from another class approached on port tack on a collision course, without bothering to look. When I finally barked 'Starboard!' to get his attention, the head of the responsible helmsman appeared from under the boom and he angrily responded: 'You have to call starboard earlier!' At another point in the same race I was sailing along a stone quay, a mere two metres away, with wind from the shore and a boat just below me. A bigger and faster boat approached from behind, clearly intending to push its way in between me and the quay. I called to the helmsman and told him he couldn't, and that he should sail under us. He stared at me as if in a trance and held his course. When he approached to within a metre of my transom I shouted again that he may not, and could not, do what he was trying. He nonetheless drove between me and the quay, and the result –

colliding with both me and the quay, and damage. The man looked furiously at me and came up with the following response: 'Yes, but my boat is faster.' Somehow he thought that was sufficient justification...

All right, let's move on to a few examples of what you can do tactically with regards to the race rules, or what you need to be aware of. Suppose that you are approaching the bottom mark and an opponent has overlapped you on the inside. Once you sail into the zone (three-boat-length circle around the mark) you have to give him room, and he'll sail ahead of you on to the upwind leg. A good solution is to come up higher before you enter the circle and sail above the zone. He is left no other option except to tack, while at that moment you gybe. As you enter the zone the situation is flipped, and as you are now the inside boat he has to give you room (Fig 53). If he doesn't tack but instead continues on above you, it doesn't make a difference. You can choose when to gybe and he'll gybe just behind or above you, and he'll have to let you go ahead or give you room at the mark.

Another example: Running downwind, you pull to within three lengths of another boat on his leeward side (an overlap now exists). In this case, you may not come up higher than your proper course, but for a good reason you want to anyway. Nothing is easier than to gybe the mainsail boom to the other side and back, while the spinnaker or whisker pole can remain in place undisturbed. The earlier same-tack situation is no longer in force, and there is a new situation where you have the right to come up higher.

Suppose once again that at the start of the last race you only have one opponent who can beat you in the standings. If he is lying starboard of the committee boat, search him

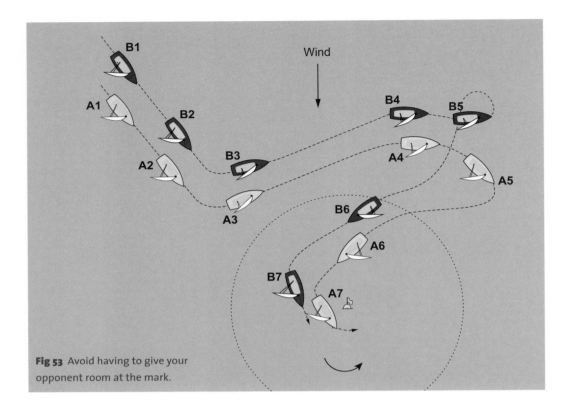

Fig 53 Avoid having to give your opponent room at the mark.

out well before the start and turn to sail below him. By luffing up, you can then bring him up past the committee boat until at some point he decides to tack, at which point you gybe or also tack to port and remain just below him. Now he can't gybe back toward the committee boat to start, and you can control him the whole time like this. You can tack back if he does, and you can repeat the same little game over and over.

An interesting possibility is when you haven't already had a bad race to use as a discard, and your opponent has (Fig 54).

Tacking at the same time is also nice. On port tack you pass behind your opponent on starboard tack. For whatever reason, your opponent tacks directly to go with you. Perhaps with the intention of holding you close, because he thinks he'll just make the mark, or whatever. If you now tack at exactly

the same moment, you create a huge problem for him, because when two boats tack at the same time, the boat that tacks from port to starboard has right of way over the other. As he can't pass behind you, he has to immediately tack back, something he is not prepared for. The result is usually a circus on the other boat – the jib is backed, the crew doesn't know what is happening and the boat comes to a full stop (Fig 55). Had Boat A not pulled out this little trick, Boat B would have covered him on port tack so that he could not turn to the mark, and B would have rounded first (or finished first if he was heading toward the starboard mark of the finish line).

You can only pull off these tricks if you have read the rules well and understand them – but be well aware that others can play with you in the same way!

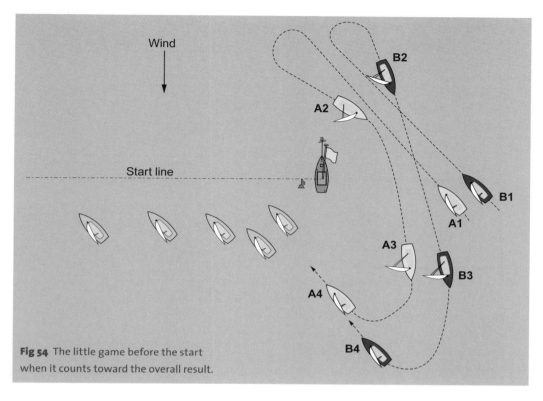

Fig 54 The little game before the start when it counts toward the overall result.

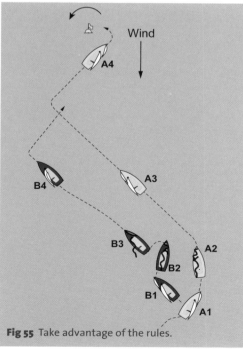

Fig 55 Take advantage of the rules.

TACTICS WITH RESPECT TO THE WIND

These are in fact dependent on the weather as discussed in Chapter 6. Let's begin by using the sine-wave pattern that the wind follows. Let's suppose that the wind shifts between 85 and 105 degrees in this cycle, with a midpoint direction of 95 degrees. With the wind between 85 and 95 degrees you make a port tack, and between 95 and 105 degrees you sail on starboard tack. In this way you'll benefit the most from the sine-wave variation in the wind and sail a shorter distance on each tack (Fig 56).

If the wind has an extremely large sine-wave variation – say, 80 to 90 degrees or more between the furthest left and right directions, then it frequently makes good sense to ease the sheets a little and bear away slightly. In this way you'll still be on the shorter path but with higher speed, and you'll reach the next shift earlier (see Fig 57). Continue to remind yourself that steering above the layline to the mark never makes sense – you just end up further away with less speed. In other words, the saying 'Take the height, because you'll need it' really makes no sense.

Of course, the same applies for a local rain shower, where the wind shifts ahead. Bear away somewhat and sail toward it on starboard tack. You'll come sooner to the wind shift and can then tack. It all fundamentally comes from the same logic – do not blindly sail as high on the wind as you can, but look ahead and think about what is going to happen. Always take advantage of a shift in the wind by being on the favoured side of the course, and by getting there as quickly as possible. Sailing big arcs at a lower speed will be your downfall in regards to your opponents, who will benefit from it handsomely.

If there is wind somewhere, always sail to it!

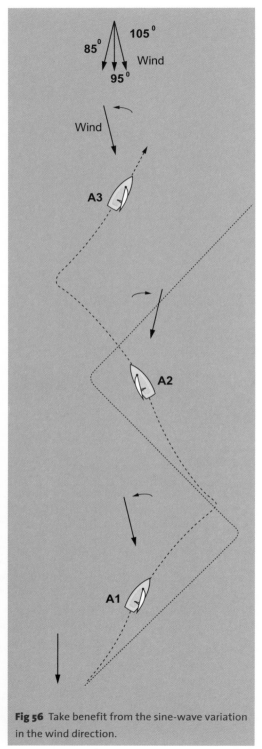
Fig 56 Take benefit from the sine-wave variation in the wind direction.

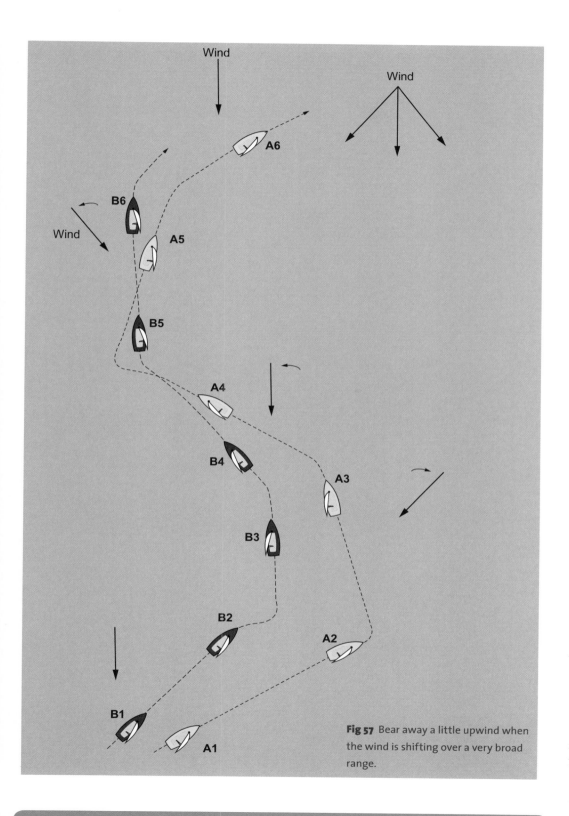

Wind

Wind

Wind

A6

B6

A5

B5

A4

B4

A3

B3

B2

A2

B1

A1

Fig 57 Bear away a little upwind when the wind is shifting over a very broad range.

protests and what they entail

EVERY SAILBOAT RACER EVENTUALLY BECOMES INVOLVED IN A PROTEST, WHETHER HE WANTS TO OR NOT. LET ME FIRST SAY THAT I'M NOT A BIG SUPPORTER OF PROTESTS WHERE IT IS UNNECESSARY, BUT THERE ARE ALWAYS CASES WHERE YOU DON'T HAVE AN OPTION. WHEN SUCH A CASE ARISES, MAKE SURE YOU DO IT WELL.

Always bear this in mind – being right, and getting the right decision, are two very different things. In a protest it is all about reaching the right decision and not about who is right. A jury will never know what really happened on the water and can only work with the facts and how they are presented to them. So stick to presenting the facts, and do not begin by telling them you are in the right – that is for them to judge.

Always avoid one thing – stating your own conclusion! It may be on the tip of your tongue at such a moment to say: 'There you are, he's lying. I'm right, he can't be telling the truth!' The jury will come to this conclusion on their own, they are there for a reason. Just give them the facts and hand them the responses (whether provoked or not) on a platter, and then look absently at the ceiling and say nothing more. They were, after all, not present for this incident, so they need to decide on the basis of the facts presented and the responses to questions posed...

If you are looking for a witness, make sure they have a reasonable and credible account. It is not the party with the most witnesses who wins, but the party with the best witness – more precisely, a witness who gives a credible account that squares with yours. Beware of producing too many witnesses, because there is a good chance they will contradict each other.

You should also be businesslike when completing the protest form. Limit it to a concise summary of the facts with a clear diagram. Don't make a drawing where it appears as if one boat must have been going three times faster than the other. Provide a summary of the facts that matches the story you will later tell the jury, and diagrams that match the situations you will imitate for the jury with little plastic boats. Through your completed protest form you give the jury a first impression, and it had better be good.

Whether you won or lost, just or unjust, thank the jury for their work and shake hands with your opponent. You'll no doubt come up against him again and it is always best to be a good sport and leave a positive impression. Grumbling or walking out angry doesn't change the situation, and it only leaves a poor impression for the next time.

QUESTIONING YOUR OPPONENT

Whether you are the protester or the subject of the protest, always exercise your right to question your opponent and witnesses. Frame your questions so that conclusions can be drawn from his responses, such that what he maintains is in fact impossible. For example:

You: Question: How far were we from the bottom mark?

Response: Around 30 to 40 metres.

Question: Had you already dropped your spinnaker?

Response: Yes.

Question: How much wind was there?

Answer: 8 to 10 knots.

Question: How long did it take for us to reach the mark?

Answer: Maybe, at the most, 5 seconds.

Question: Were we already in the zone (three-boat-length circle around the mark)?

Answer: Yes.

Question: How long is our boat?

Answer: 7 metres.

Question: So you're saying that running with a wind speed of 8 to 10 knots, or 4 to 5 metres/sec, within 5 seconds we reached a mark 30 or 40 metres away?

Answer: Ahhh, er, ... yes, I mean, um...

Thank you, I have no further questions.

QUESTIONING A WITNESS:

Question to a witness: So you are saying that I was the most inside boat on the rounding, and I touched the buoy?

Witness: Yes.

Question: Was there a boat above me that had to give me room?

Witness: Yes.

Question: Where were you at that moment?

Witness: Above and outside the other boat, because I had to give him room.

Question: How did I touch the buoy – with my sail, boom, hull or what?

Witness: Um, I think with your hull.

Question: And where were you sitting on your boat, at that moment?

Witness: I was on the foredeck, taking the spinnaker pole down.

Question: Had you already hoisted or unfurled your jib or genoa?

Witness: Yes.

Question: So you could see through your own genoa, through the sails of the boat between us, through my sails and my hull, to see me touching the buoy with my hull?

Witness: Ummm....

Thank you, no further questions.

the psychology of sailboat racing

PSYCHOLOGY BECOMES MORE AND MORE IMPORTANT IN SAILBOAT RACING, AS THE DIFFERENCE IN BOAT SPEED IS NEGLIGIBLE AT THE TOP IN INTERNATIONAL RACES. YOUR MENTAL CONDITION BECOMES AT LEAST AS IMPORTANT AS YOUR PHYSICAL, OR EVEN MORE! BUT HOW CAN YOU TRAIN IT?

It's really the same in every sport: the higher the level, the more important the state of mind becomes. Sailboat racing is no different. It starts with learning other things, such as boat handling, trimming, the rules of racing, meteorology, sailing in current and so forth. But once you reach the top 10 or 5 on the international level, then psychology begins to play an even bigger role. The top race sailors master trimming, boat handling etc to the finest detail; they all have the best equipment; but after that ... it's all about what's between your ears. Mental coaching becomes important, something that even today is highly undervalued in many countries. The subconscious begins to play a role. A racing sailor who doesn't really have a clear and relaxed mind frequently fails to recognise a cloud that brings a wind shift, or see a tide transition line ahead. He's not thinking about how an opponent will react if he gybes or tacks. In short, he misses things and can no longer influence his competitors, much less control them. He needs self-confidence and the belief he can outwit his opponents.

I'll give a few examples, but it is then up to you, the reader, to take them on board and to recognise your own weaknesses.

Long ago, during an Olympics campaign, my biggest competitor was completely preoccupied with running his own company. During the selection races the first race was always a cakewalk for me, because at this time he was easy to beat. The difference was that he was unconsciously still thinking about work, while on Friday morning I was already unwinding at the harbour. It also put him off a little to have to rig his boat while I relaxed outside a café, reading the newspaper and drinking coffee. Of course, you need to recognise that everyone is different, and has different ways to get comfortable in their own skin. Some need a kick of adrenaline to wake up and sail a good race, others seek true relaxation before they can perform well. It is therefore very important to know what works best for you and your crew.

I also coached a women's team in an Olympics campaign. They had the right experience, and had just missed a medal in the previous Olympics due to one of the crew falling ill. They had perfect boat handling, great boat speed, and so on – in short, all the

Mentally strong and highly focused.

ingredients were there for a successful campaign. But there was one real problem: they were too nice to their opponents and lacked just a little self-confidence. In short, their fighting spirit was broken.

During a major international series they were well positioned going into the medal race. I racked my brain how I could get the helmswoman fully engaged in the last race – a short race where a good start (a weaker point for her) was essential. The only opportunity to try to make her more aggressive was during the lunch break. I began to more or less challenge her, and told her that the medal race didn't make real sense for her and she should haul her boat out now while the crane wasn't busy. I also told her she should call her parents and tell

them not to come after all, since it would be a long drive to the race location for what would turn out to be a huge disappointment. And so I continued to egg her on, until she suddenly stood up, red-faced, and slapped me across the face in public. I finally got her where she needed to be!

On the way to the start I said little to her and just shrugged my shoulders when she spoke. The result? She was so angry that she made a world-class start and gloriously won the medal race. After it was over she came to me and asked: 'Did you mean everything you said during lunch, or did you have another motive?' I then openly explained why I did it, and that it fortunately worked.

But this can also backfire completely. Sometimes it is better to take someone you

The blue boat hadn't counted on this.

are coaching out for a beer, and in this way ensure they are completely relaxed. Everybody reacts differently and it is up to the coach to discover which approach will get someone into their comfort zone and ready to perform optimally. Fostering genuine self-confidence – not to be confused with bravado – is very important.

Further, there are a few obvious things that always work in large race fleets. Sailors allow themselves to be unconsciously intimidated by boats that look aggressive and have professional appearances. Just because of the colour of a boat, decals, matching branded gear for the crew and so on, a number of competitors will keep clear of it at the start or during the race.

Getting your boat in the water in a timely fashion, so that you are sitting back with a cup of coffee while others are still busy setting up and rigging their boats, will give you a psychological advantage. It may sound exaggerated, but it really works – for you but also against your opponents. In fact, it helps you impose your will on them without them realising it. They will try to avoid boat-to-boat battles with you. You know how to undermine their confidence, and you make them nervous so that they make poor decisions and mistakes. Above all, it gives your own self-confidence a boost, and promotes sufficient inner calm so that you will be sharp and make proper decisions during the race.

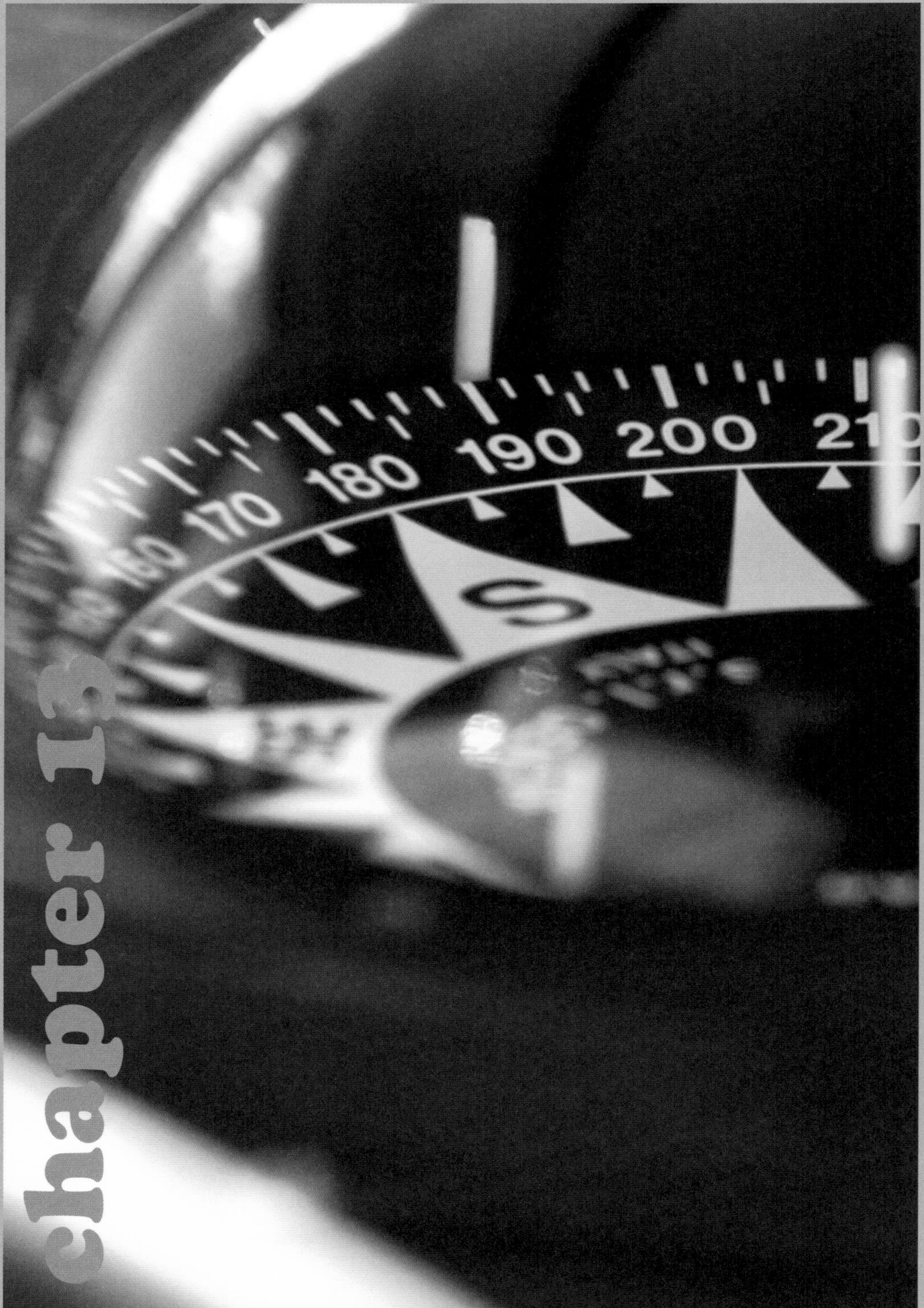

chapter 13

instruments

FOR MANY (RACING) SAILORS THE INSTRUMENTS, PRIMARILY THE ELECTRONICS, REPRESENT THE MOST SOUGHT-AFTER TOYS TO HAVE ON BOARD. WHEN IT COMES TO METERS AND ANTENNAS, THE MORE THE BETTER! THE VALUE OF THESE PLAYTHINGS IS NOT ALWAYS ENTIRELY CLEAR TO ME.

I have seen GPS displays on a 2.4mR, a one-man boat that is 4.2m in length, to measure speed and to trim on that basis. If you consider the 2.4m sails upwind at around 3 knots (and rarely 4 knots), and the difference between sailing hard on the wind and not is around 1% ... try to determine this using a GPS. You don't know if you are sailing 1 or a half degree higher or lower, and whether adjusting the trim truly gives you a better VMG (velocity made good, your speed in the direction of the mark) on a tack.

In one-design classes I feel that there is only one good way to assess trim and VMG, and that is with a sparring partner. For offshore yachts this is a little more difficult as they sail at different speeds, and in this case there are few real alternatives to using instruments. But even then...

The problem is that instruments can't think, but fortunately people can. Around thirty years ago, on the big boats that I periodically sailed on, there were already computers on board that gave advice based on the boat's polar diagrams. They warned you, for example, that a few hundred metres before the top mark you would need to change down from the #2 genoa to the #3, because your heel angle was 2 degrees too much. The stupid thing couldn't figure out that changing the headsail would cost a few minutes, while continuing a few hundred metres further with 2 degrees excessive heel would cost only a few seconds.

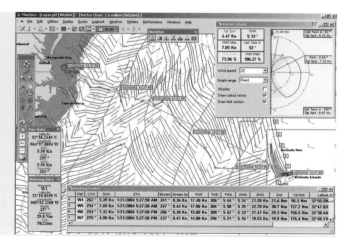

The same thing happened when GPS instruments were introduced. In a cross current, that clever little box tried to get you to steer in a straight line over the ground to the next mark, but instead you sailed a big comma-shape through the water, and sometimes lost hours on the last part as you fought against the current (indeed, you still see this happen nowadays). OK, you can argue that you can look at the course over ground to determine how much to compensate for the current, but the instruments don't know if the wind or current will increase or decrease, or change direction, and how to compensate for it.

The next development was to integrate weather forecasts into this sacred box. This is also nice, but the box can't see clouds, rain showers, shore effects, or the other boats. What *you* can see and interpret in the near term is still very essential.

The same applies to the wind direction and wind speed meters. A change in the wind reaches the luff of the genoa before it gets to the thing at the top of the mast. Further, the wind speed and direction are constantly affected by the movement of the mast top over waves. In short, steering by instruments is much less advantageous than steering by telltales and the heel angle.

Then you have the polar diagrams and grib files, that all too often push you toward an extreme (but not necessarily optimal or correct) choice. Do the polar diagrams take into account if you are sailing on flat water, or in steep waves? No, they are an average case. Do they know if you are sailing singlehanded, or with ten crew sitting on the rail? This also makes quite a difference with regards to sail selection and heel angle. Nor do the grib files tell you if a land or sea breeze is coming, or if you have to account for a shore effect.

Should you throw all of your instruments overboard? No, of course not. They can be very handy, but always bear in mind that they are nothing more than aids that can frequently give you indications and assist you. Especially realise that they are not sacred; they can't think, that is still something you have to do. They are in fact glorified calculators that perform probability calculations, and as with any probability calculation it gives you an average probability. As long as you realise that averages only come about by considering outlying points from above and below, you'll be fine – you can then make your own adjustments based on observations and logical thinking. Give instruments and on-board computers the place they deserve, no more and no less.

chapter 14

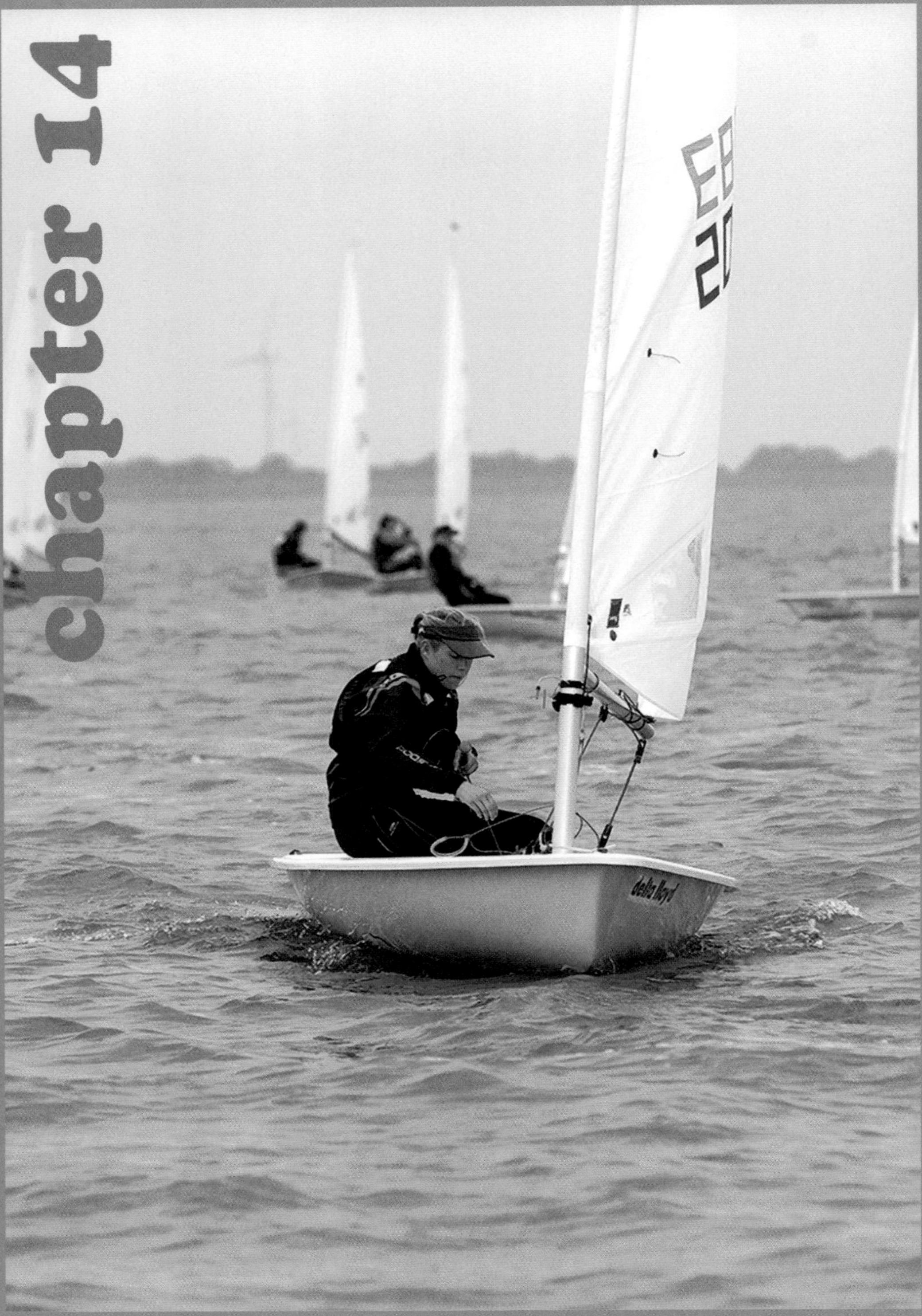

how sails work

THE TITLE OF THIS CHAPTER COULD JUST AS EASILY HAVE BEEN: 'WHY DOES A SAILBOAT GO FORWARD WHEN SAILING UPWIND, INSTEAD OF BACKWARD AND LEEWARD?' OF COURSE, AS A RACING SAILOR YOU WOULD LIKE TO HEAR HOW YOU CAN GET THE MOST OUT OF YOUR MOTOR (THE SAILS). HOWEVER, TO OPTIMALLY TUNE THE MOTOR YOU FIRST NEED TO UNDERSTAND HOW IT WORKS, AND HOW IT DRIVES AHEAD WITH THE FUEL (THE WIND). TO UNDERSTAND THIS, YOU NEED A LITTLE BIT OF THEORY – BUT JUST AS I NOTED AT THE BEGINNING OF THE BOOK, ONLY THEORY THAT YOU AS A RACE SAILOR CAN ACTUALLY WORK WITH! THE REAL QUESTION IS: HOW CAN YOU TRIM YOUR SAILS IF YOU DON'T KNOW HOW THEY WORK OR PROVIDE OPTIMAL DRIVE? A LITTLE MORE TO CHEW ON – SO TRY TO UNDERSTAND THE UNDERLYING THEORY.

In principle, you can consider a sail as a wing that is put into an airflow, so many principles of a sail can be explained by the well-known principles of a wing. There are also some important differences. A sail, as compared to a wing, is very thin all over the whole surface and more flexible, but for our purposes this has no real consequences.

Additionally, the sail is used in situations where a normal wing is not employed – think about when the sail is set at 90 degrees to the wind when sailing downwind. Finally, the shape of the sail is greatly determined by the user (the sailor), who can make significant changes to the profile (the cross section of the sail), the depth (luff tension, foot tension, mast bend, sail batten tension and so on), and to the position of the sail relative to the wind ('angle of entry') along the full height of the sail – in other words, the sail twist.

In practice, as well as predicted by theoretical physics, how a body reacts when placed in the flow of a liquid (water) or gas (air) is well understood. There is always a force acting against the body when there is an underlying difference in speeds between the flow and the body. This is called 'drag', a force opposite to the direction of motion. In nature, every motion gives rise to drag. Just as we already saw with the forces acting on the sails, sheets and blocks, the size of the force of drag is also directly proportional to the square of the speed of the body within the flow.

It further turns out that, provided that the body is given the proper shape, a force can be generated perpendicular to the flow. This force is called 'lift'. In practice this has a range of useful applications, such as the lift from the wings on an aeroplane that allows the aeroplane to fly. Lift is also used to steer a boat (the rudder) and to drive it through the water (the propeller). In reality, the propeller is nothing more than a set of wings on a shaft that generate lift to propel the boat forward. And last but not least, the sails, which are of course also intended to drive the boat forward.

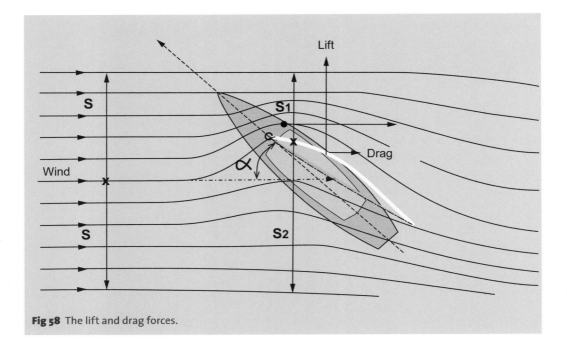

Fig 58 The lift and drag forces.

Let's now look from above at the horizontal cross section of a sail on a boat (Fig 58). A sail is set at an angle with respect to the undisturbed wind – what exactly happens now? The undisturbed wind streams from the left at a certain speed. The lines as drawn are called the 'lines of flow'; these are the paths the air particles follow in a stationary flow. The air particles cannot leave these paths in a stationary flow. Because a sail placed in this airflow disturbs these paths, the air particles need to find a way around it. Either through measurement or by calculation, the resulting lines of flow, as shown in the drawing, can be determined. It now appears that the flow around the wing (the sail) has split into two parts; one part travels along the lee side of the sail and the other along the windward side.

In the drawing we also see that the lines of flow on the leeward side of the boat are brought closer together from S to S1; on the windward side the lines of flow are spread out from S to S2. For the type of flow we are currently examining, there is a law of fluid dynamics, which states that flow is faster if the lines of flow come closer together and slowed if the lines are spread further out. This is called the 'Law of Continuity' and applies with respect to the speed in an undisturbed flow. We can therefore ascertain that on the lee of the sail, at point S1, the flow is accelerated and on the windward side, at point S2, the flow is slowed down.

A second law, 'Bernoulli's Law', also applies in this type of flow. It states that as the speed of the flow is increased (relative to the undisturbed flow), its pressure decreases, and the converse. Conclusion: in the cross section a lower pressure prevails at S1 and a higher pressure at S2, as compared to the undisturbed flow. We can reproduce this view for several locations along the length of the sail, in each case yielding a difference in pressure between the lee side of the sail and the weather side. Further, we also know that pressure over a

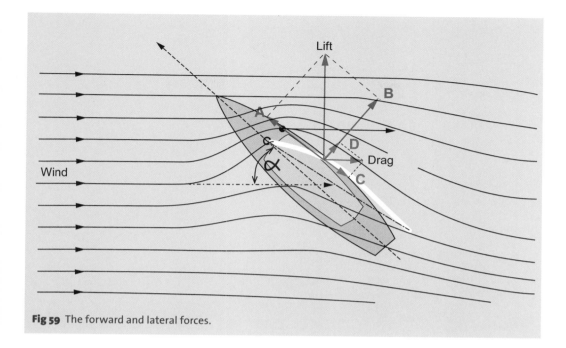

Fig 59 The forward and lateral forces.

surface yields a force, and therefore there is a total force perpendicular to the sailcloth. We can separate this force vector into two components, one perpendicular to the direction of the undisturbed flow (lift) and one in the direction of the flow (drag).

In Fig 59 we resolve the lift vector into a force A along the centreline of the boat, and B perpendicular to it. We can also resolve the drag into force C along the centreline of the boat, and force D perpendicular to it. What we now see is that the forward force is the result of subtracting C from A. The only problem is we are left with a perpendicular force, the sum of vectors B and D, but we can compensate for this lateral force by way of a centreboard or a keel. When pushed to leeward, the centreboard or keel delivers a windward force through the water. In this way we avoid too much leeway as we sail forward. But we encounter another problem – the lateral forces B plus D from the sail, and the windward force on the lee side of the

centreboard or keel, act as levers and deliver torque that acts to capsize the boat. To counter this we bring the crew weight to windward, and/or have ballast in the keel. In this way we create a counter-torque – which provides the stability.

Fig 60 shows the distribution of pressure across the sail, where we see that the biggest differences in pressure develop in the forward part of the sail. We can further see from the direction of the arrows that the forward part of the sail delivers the most lift, and very little drag.

The example described here is valid for a specific position of the sail relative to the undisturbed flow. Should this position – the angle of entry of the flow over a wing or sail – be changed, then the forces on the sail will also be changed. Both the lift and drag are affected by this angle and, perhaps even more important, their mutual relationship (ratio of one to the other) also changes when changing the angle. For wings, and thus also for sails,

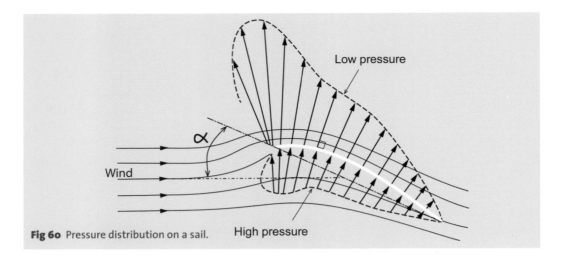

Fig 60 Pressure distribution on a sail.

Low pressure

High pressure

Wind

the change in lift and drag over a range of angles is shown in the so-called polar plot (not to be confused with the polar diagram for the boat). The magnitude and direction of the lift and drag are shown over the complete range of angles of entry between the wind and the sail, that is to say, from 0 degrees (directly into the wind) to 90 degrees (perpendicular to the sail, as when running dead downwind). An example of this plot is provided in Fig 61.

Lift is plotted along the vertical axis and drag along the horizontal axis. The coefficients are 'dimensionless', which means that for a sail with identical shape (and for any surface area A, and any wind speed V) the lift and drag can be calculated. The angle of entry for the sail is noted at points along the polar curve. This is the most often used way to characterise wings (and therefore sails), and provides a simple and

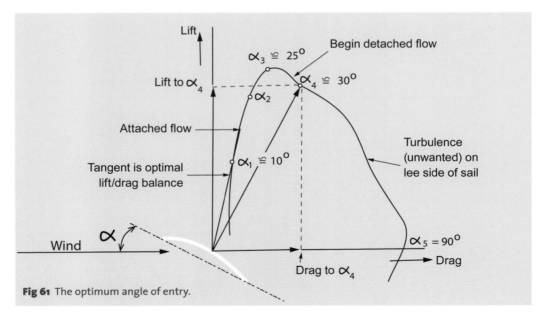

Fig 61 The optimum angle of entry.

easy manner to compare them. The angles of entry at different points are noted along the curve.

A few things come out immediately from this: at an angle of attack of 0 degrees (wind from directly in front of the sail) there is no lift and only drag. This is in part because the sail is flapping and can't provide any lift (different from a rigid wing!). At an angle of 90 degrees to the sail we also only see drag. This occurs when running dead downwind, where the boom is squared off to the point that it is limited by the shrouds.

We further see that at smaller angles of entry (between 10 and 20 degrees) the lift is relatively large as compared to the drag. This is the range for points of sail from close to the wind, to eased off, up to and including a beam reach. With a relatively small change in the position of the boom (by mainsheet or traveller) we can effect a big change in these forces. With angles of entry greater than 30 degrees, the force of the lift decreases dramatically while the drag continues to increase. Here we see the airflow detaching from the lee side of the sail; the wind no longer follows the paths shown in Fig 58, but looks increasingly like in Fig 62. In fact the profile is stalled, and the telltales on the lee side of the sail will only dance in the turbulence. This is at the expense of lift as well as drag.

It is important, of course, also to realise that it is ultimately not the lift and drag that count, but the resolved forces that act along the length of the boat (longitudinally) and laterally to it (Fig 59). The longitudinal force (the propulsive force) – that's what it's all about. The lateral force only causes leeway. The longitudinal force is our forward drive and should be maximised; the higher the force, the higher the speed we can achieve. It is clear from the above that this is not only dependent on the angle of entry relative to the boat, but also the angle of the sail on the boat, and consequently the angle of entry of the wind on the sail.

Depending on the apparent wind angle, it is important to attach greater or lesser importance to lift or drag respectively (see

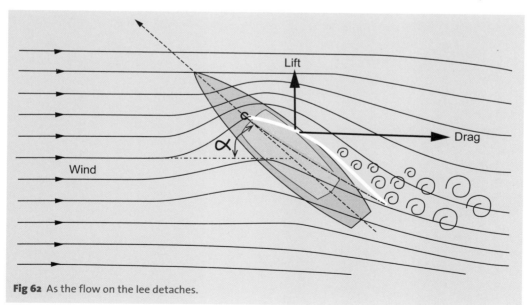

Fig 62 As the flow on the lee detaches.

Fig 63). When sailing to windward it is important to have as much lift as possible, with the least possible drag. The forward force is generated by the lift, and can easily be four or five times greater than the drag. This is fortunate, because in this case the drag is counterproductive; the longitudinal component of the drag is opposite the direction of travel. The total lateral force on the sails is also large and this can result in a significant heel, which is unfavourable with regards to the drag from the hull through the water. You need to trim as necessary to reduce the heel, but without affecting the forward drive.

With wind on the beam, the forward drive comes completely from lift, and drag plays a subordinate role. In this case it is also important to generate as much lift from the sails as possible. This can include trimming the sails fuller. On the jib or genoa this happens automatically if you ease the sheets to the point just before the luff begins to shudder. A fuller profile delivers more lift than a flatter profile. This can be seen in Fig 64, a polar diagram where the lift and drag are given for three different depths for the sail (a is 5%, b is 10% and c is 15% depth). In particular, it is clearly apparent that for a beam reach, where the sail works best at a 10 to 20 degree angle of entry, there is much to be gained with a fuller sail.

This figure also shows the situation when dead downwind. It is clear the forward drive is delivered exclusively by the drag, and the lift doesn't contribute at all. Further, you can see that there is a minimal difference between a fuller or flatter sail. Clearly the forward drive can also be improved by not sailing directly downwind but at a slight angle (crossing downwind). The lift that is generated in that way can provide additional forward drive (in conjunction with the drag).

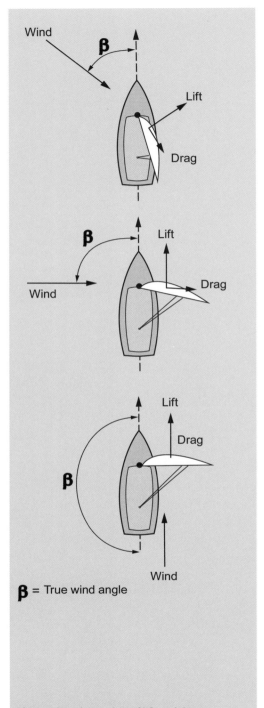

β = True wind angle

Fig 63 The relationship of lift and drag at different points of sail.

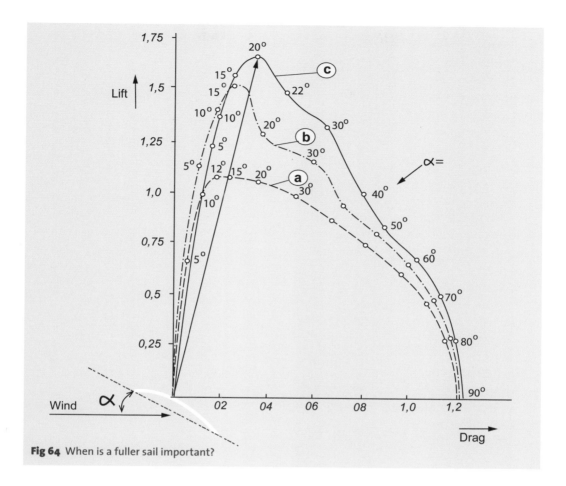

Fig 64 When is a fuller sail important?

The amount of additional benefit from this largely depends on the type of boat and the wind force. It will be less beneficial for heavier boats (like sailing barges) than for lighter boats and catamarans – for the latter it is really a 'must do'! Not to mention iceboats, which cross downwind and reach speeds many times higher than the true wind speed.

Up to now we have only spoken about a single sail. However, sail plans are usually combinations of a mainsail and a jib or genoa. This has a huge influence on the lift and drag of the sails. One of the major benefits of a foresail is that there are additional benefits to dividing the pressure between the two sails.

The proper alignment of the two sails will improve flow over the mainsail where it may have been stalled otherwise, especially when sailing at slightly larger wind angles. Even more important is the change in the flow patterns when the two sails are set close to each other in tighter wind angles, such as beating upwind (Fig 65). In this drawing, the pressure divided between the two sails is first shown as if the two sails were working separately (a and a), and then for the case that they are set closely and working together (b and c). It is clear that the pressure on the forward sail sharply increases (providing more lift), while the pressure on the rear sail decreases. The decrease in pressure on the

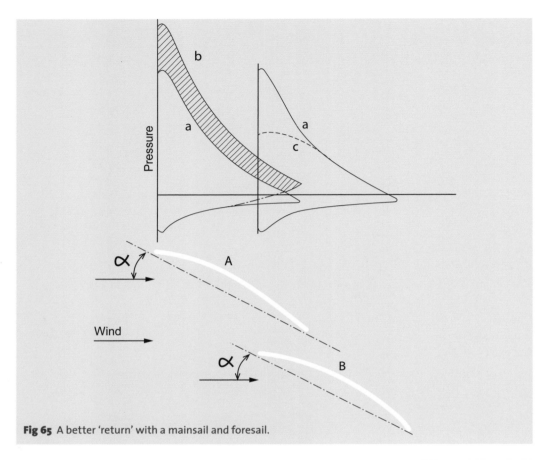

Fig 65 A better 'return' with a mainsail and foresail.

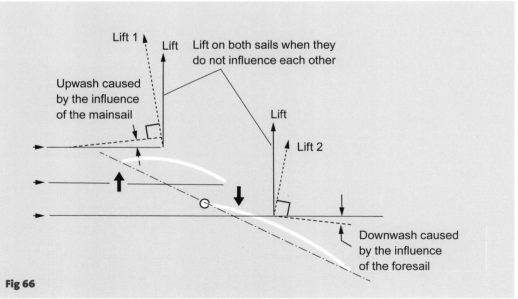

Fig 66

rear sail is less than the increase in pressure on the forward sail (see drawing); compare the area of a (foresail) plus a (mainsail) with the combined area of b (foresail) and c (mainsail)! Contrary to what is commonly believed, it is not the mainsail that is providing the most drive, but the foresail – in short, the combination delivers more force than the sum of the two separate parts!

This is again apparent in Fig 66, where two sails are set closely together. This is because of complex phenomena on and around sails due to their mutual interaction (like the so-called upwash), which I won't go into further here. What is important to remember is that the interaction is significant and it is mainly to the benefit of the foresail. The frequently cited 'slot effect', where the flow between the foresail and the mainsail is accelerated, does not exist – in reality the opposite is true!

I hope these theoretical explanations about how sails work have given you more insight into how forces on the sails develop, and how they then generate the forward drive. I also hope to have succeeded in outlining the very complicated and delicate balance that ultimately determines the speed of a boat on different points of sail. Of course, in the framework of this book I really had to limit myself! There is really so much more to say, and this could fill many more books. But I didn't want to bother you with unnecessary theory – do you still remember?

On the basis of the foregoing, you now understand how the motor (the sails) works, and with the benefit of logical thinking you can begin to tune (trim) the motor on different legs. Wildly pulling trim lines with the hope of going faster – from now on, this belongs to the past!

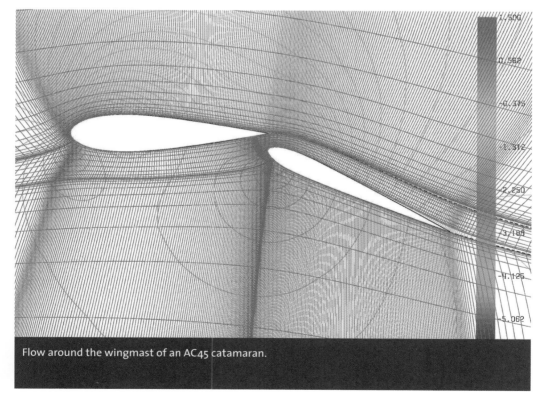

Flow around the wingmast of an AC45 catamaran.

afterword

HOPEFULLY WITH THIS BOOK I'VE SUCCEEDED IN GETTING POTENTIAL SAILBOAT RACERS TO THINK – ABOUT HOW COMPLICATED IT IS, BUT ALSO HOW LOGICAL AND ENJOYABLE RACING CAN REALLY BE.

In my view, the most important thing to learn in sailboat racing is still the following: first teach yourself a proper logical manner of thinking, and then constantly work through changing situations without getting stressed out. Speak with your crew; discuss various situations and changes in the weather that may occur. Make a strategic and tactical plan before the start, where you consider your place in the standings, clouds, shore effects, current and so forth, giving a relative weighting to each – because there are always conflicting factors! Ensure that one of the elements of this plan is the moment that you have to go to plan B, if one of the identified factors radically changes.

It may have been dizzying in the beginning when you realised everything you needed to think about, but that will gradually disappear as you gain experience. Then it will become even more fun. Remember to put aside unnecessary things or less important details, and set priorities honestly and objectively. In this way you'll learn a little faster, achieve results sooner, and save yourself a lot of time and unnecessary effort.

further reading

Skipper's Cockpit Racing Guide:
For dinghies, keelboats and yachts
ISBN: 9781472900319
Tim Davison

The *Skipper's Cockpit Racing Guide* is
an at-a-glance reference for dinghy
and yacht racers, covering everything
they need to know to improve their
performance – and win. From those in
their first year of racing to old hands
wondering why they're not winning,
this splash-proof, lie-flat guide covers
an enormous amount of detail in a
simple, easy to follow format. Topics
cover everything from setting goals and assembling the right gear, through to
starting, strategy, and the rules of the race. A final section on troubleshooting
enables you to rate your performance and identify areas for improvement.

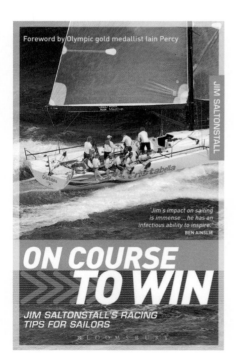

On Course to Win: Jim Saltonstall's Racing
Tips for Sailors
ISBN: 9781408187869
Jim Saltonstall

This quick reference handbook distills the wisdom
of Jim Saltonstall's 40 years in the business coaching
multiple National, European, World and Olympic
racing champions, to help all dinghy, yacht and
windsurfers to improve their performance in one of
the most challenging sports in the world. Featuring
photographs that illustrate specific aspects of all
races and a checklist of all the key issues racers need
to think about as they progress around the course,
On Course to Win intelligently analyses all the issues
that can arise at any point on the racecourse.

Fast Handling Technique
ISBN: 9781408154168
Frank Bethwaite

Budding racers of all levels will welcome this
unique book as a godsend. This book is a scientific
analysis of what makes fast sailors fast. Making
use of video cameras aligned to GPS read-outs to
track the fastest racers, Bethwaite meticulously
analyses what winners do and how they do it, to
show the rest of us how to get the best out of a
racing craft. It informs, instructs and enables
everyone to employ the techniques of the most
successful racers, and make racing more
competitive for participants, and more exciting
for those of us watching.

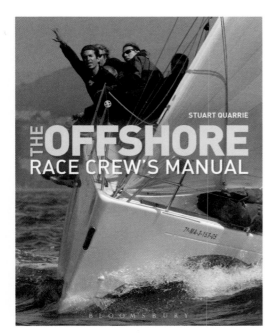

The Offshore Race Crew's Manual
ISBN: 9781408157282
Stuart Quarrie

Success in any yacht race depends to a large
degree on the ability of the crew to perform
any boat-handling manoeuvre faultlessly and
speedily. This book explains the evolution of
just about every situation that is likely to be
encountered during a race at sea. Each one is
presented with an overview of the sequence
that should take place and its objective, then
the task of each crew member is explained for
its preparation, operation and completion.
Photographs and illustrations clarify what
are often complex situations.

High Performance Sailing: Faster Racing Techniques 2nd edition
ISBN: 9781408124918
Frank Bethwaite

Some people like to sail. Some people like to sail fast. This is a book about sailing faster. During the past few decades there has been a revolution in the way some boat designers and sailors have thought about, designed, built and sailed their boats. This ground-breaking reference book is about the new ideas which have led to these greater speeds and the faster sailing techniques which have been developed to achieve them. This is the bible for racing sailors of all levels and abilities from dinghies through to America's Cup.

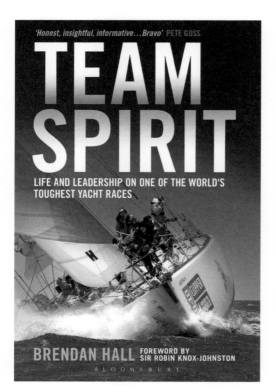

Team Spirit: Life and Leadership on One of the World's Toughest Yacht Races
ISBN: 9781408187999
Brendan Hall

The Clipper Round the World Yacht Race is the ultimate long distance challenge – a 35,000-mile circumnavigation of the globe, contested by amateur crews in identical racing yachts. Taking part in it requires incredible teamwork, leadership, skill, courage and focus. Winning it is a whole different game. *Team Spirit* is the compelling story of a race on the edge, a young skipper's crash-course in leadership under gruelling pressure, and a determined journey to triumph against the odds.

index

Page numbers in *italic* refer to Figures